Seeing Again for the first time

Mindful Communication in the Age of Distraction.

Josh Misner, PhD

Cover created by Corey Jeppesen. © Corey Jeppesen.

Kendall Hunt
publishing company

www.kendallhunt.com
Send all inquiries to:
4050 Westmark Drive
Dubuque, IA 52004-1840

Copyright © 2017 by Kendall Hunt Publishing Company

ISBN 978-1-5249-4949-5

All rights reserved. No part of this publication may be reproduced, stored in a retrieval system, or transmitted, in any form or by any means, electronic, mechanical, photocopying, recording, or otherwise, without the prior written permission of the copyright owner.

Published in the United States of America

DEDICATION

To my partner in life, Stacie, I thank you for being my reality check. This book would never have been written without you having the courage and strength to challenge me and wake me up to all the possibilities of life, especially when it seemed like I would have much rather stayed in my bubble of delusion. We both now know that growth and development is a painful and difficult journey, but there is nobody else in the world with whom I would have rather taken the journey.

To my children, your grace and presence have taught me the value of mindfulness. Through our interactions, I discover joy, and being your father has been the greatest accomplishment of my life.

To the countless other mentors along the way—Shann Ray, Thich Nhat Hanh, and Dr. Bellini, to name a few—your priceless guidance set me on the path toward mindfulness, and I hope this book pays that forward for others. Your lessons live on, and your wisdom continues to make a tremendous impact on the lives and relationships of so many.

Contents

Introduction — Seeing Again for the First Time … vii

PART 1 · Mindful Awareness … 1

- Chapter 1 Introduction to Mindfulness and the Age of Distraction … 3
- Chapter 2 Paying Attention with Purpose … 13
- Chapter 3 Perception of Self and Perceptions of Others … 21
- Chapter 4 Learning to Be Alone … 29

PART 2 · Resilience … 37

- Chapter 5 Judgment, Critique, and Ego … 39
- Chapter 6 The Poison of Pride and the Antidote of Forgiveness … 45
- Chapter 7 Listening—The Greater Half of Communication … 55
- Chapter 8 Vulnerability and Accountability … 65

PART 3 · Savoring … 75

- Chapter 9 Savoring the Moment … 77
- Chapter 10 Must Be Present to Win … 87
- Chapter 11 Cultivating Gratitude … 101
- Chapter 12 Appreciation—The Outward Expression of Gratitude … 107

PART 4 · Connecting … 115

- Chapter 13 Linking Humility with Gratitude … 117
- Chapter 14 In the Service of Others … 121
- Chapter 15 Question Everything … 131

Conclusion … 145

Introduction—Seeing Again for the First Time

In 2010, as part of a doctoral class project, I was assigned to interview someone for the purpose of learning how to conduct qualitative research. Part of the project was to conduct this interview with someone I knew, based on a topic related to my area of research interest. At that time, I knew I was interested in researching more about the impact of mindfulness on interpersonal relationships, but I wasn't exactly certain as to what context I wanted to use for that research, so I played it safe by interviewing a friend about his experiences in fatherhood. One of my questions was related to something my friend had previously described regarding how he and his child frequently had moments where it seemed like the world would gradually disappear and they found themselves alone together in a place where neither persons nor things could possibly distract them away from the magic of the moment.

I pressed further into the interview with my friend, prodding him about this curious statement that had piqued my interest. "Tell me more about those moments when it seems like the world disappears, leaving behind only you and your child," I asked. His response was worded so perfectly, yet so curiously, that it was as though he had fired some imaginary starter pistol that would set me off on my life's work.

He stated, *"It's almost as though I'm seeing her again for the first time."*

I was floored by this simple response. Its depth and beauty so perfectly described what happens whenever we surrender ourselves to the power of a moment spent interacting with someone we love. In moments like these, it is as though layer after layer of grime and fuzziness are stripped away in an instant, immersing us within a state of perfect clarity, and yet, all we see then is the interaction in front of us as if it was all that has ever mattered or ever will matter.

Everything in such a moment is fresh and new, even if we have seen or experienced those things a thousand times before. Such moments define the heart of mindful presence.

This book may be unlike other books; when I set out to write this book, my goal was to create an immersive, interactive, and, dare I say, *intimate* experience between you, the reader, and this text. It has long been my view that books are meant to be *felt* as they are experienced by readers, but far too many books fail to leave us with an impression because they fail on so many levels to connect to that which generates feelings like the mindful interaction my friend had previously described.

Therefore, based on this view, my task, as the author, is to give you, the reader, a rich and full experience as you navigate this book. You will do more than simply read and reflect as you embark on a journey into the realm of mindful interpersonal communication. Theories must leave the page and find their place in the real world for them to have value, so this book will, in many ways, act as a guide to applying these theories to your everyday interaction. There will be times when this book will become a physical prop in intricate social experiments designed to help you break out of self-imposed limitations. Other times, you will be required to put some yourself into the book as well, leaving an indelible mark behind, chronicling that portion of your journey.

This book will make you think. It will frustrate you and make you angry in certain points. It may very well make you cry at other times. Sometimes, those tears will be drawn from a well of despair or frustration. Other times, those tears might be a fountain of joy and fullness. Ultimately, as you close the book for the last time, if I have achieved the goal that I set out to achieve as I sank into the cushions of my living room sofa to commence writing it on a cold November evening, then the act of setting down the book for the last time may feel less like relief for having completed a long read and more like a bittersweet departure, the parting of ways between you and your loved one, not knowing when you will see one another again. If this sounds like a lofty goal, it is.

What to Expect

This book is divided into four major parts, each of which has four chapters. It is specifically and methodically designed so that each chapter builds upon the last, and each part fits together like a puzzle. In the end, you will have a more complete picture of what it means to be a more mindful communicator.

Each chapter includes an activity that, in many cases, will involve physically interacting with this book. At some points, you may be required to write in the book, so have a pen or pencil handy. At other points, the interaction may involve more of a pleasantly destructive interaction with the pages, at which point, be brave, but take care so as not to damage the reading that still lay ahead of you. In any case, be sure to do the activities, and as you do them, understand that the more of yourself that you put into the activities, the more you will get out of them. If you take the activities to heart and engage in them with both courage and reckless abandon, then they will become powerful tools to carve you into a model of mindful communication.

However, not all of the activities will be profound or life-altering. Some activities may resonate more with certain people than with others, so if you do an activity and put mindful effort into it, don't be disappointed if your first reaction is more like, "Meh . . ." Also, not all of the activities produce rainbows featuring unicorns being ridden by cute, fuzzy kittens. Some of the activities may go to a dark place, the kind of shadowy realm of self-reflection you likely would rather avoid if you could help it—but do so with courage. As mentioned previously, each piece of the puzzle forms an important part of the bigger picture, so trust in the process and keep moving forward. By the end of this book, if you have done each and every activity mindfully and faithfully, then you will have grown and developed tremendously as a communicator, but more than that, you *will* be able to see tangible, visible, and even measurable results immediately.

Without further ado, let us begin . . .

PART 1
Mindful Awareness

In the first leg of our four-part journey, we will spend the next four chapters looking inward, at how intrapersonal communication (communication within ourselves, better known as thought) affects the way in which we interact with the world around us. Our goals for this first part of the book are as follows:

- To identify the difficulties with controlling our thought processes;
- To describe the extent to which we control our thoughts;
- To identify barriers to clearing the mind in preparation for listening;
- To practice nurturing mindfulness through various activities;
- To identify, define, and describe behaviors characterizing a mindful state of mind;
- To discover how others view our communication habits;
- To explore the need to be alone and to unwind; and
- To articulate our communication styles based on self-reflection.

CHAPTER 1

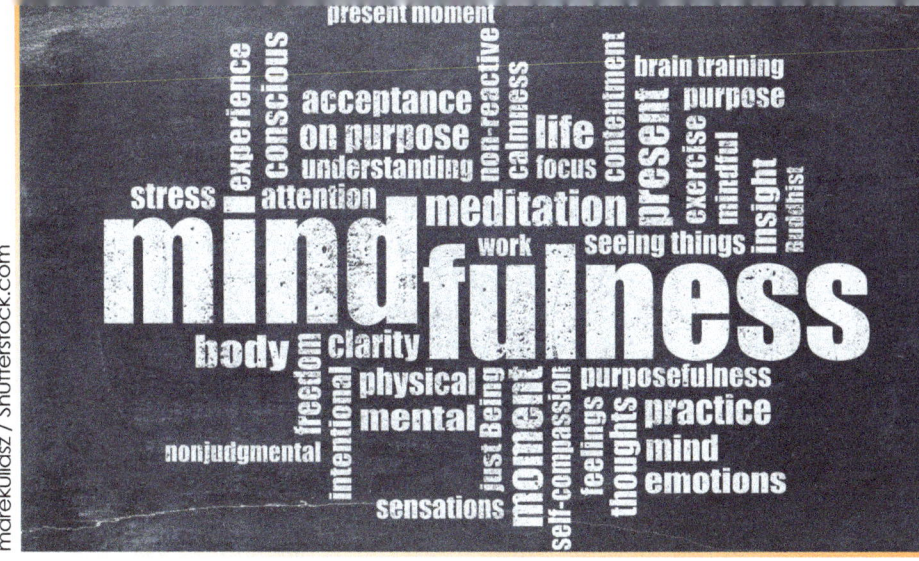

Introduction to Mindfulness and the Age of Distraction

What is Mindfulness?

Clinical psychologist and world-renowned mindfulness researcher, Jon Kabat Zinn, once said that being mindful was simply the act of paying attention on purpose. Taking this definition a few steps further, Harvard Psychologist Ellen Langer stated that mindfulness is comprised of four major components:

- Present-centered awareness
- Intention
- The ability to notice that which is new within the moment
- Nonjudgmental acceptance of whatever arises in the moment

Breaking these four components down further, we can better understand what these qualities are by actually examining what they are *not*.

Present-centered awareness implies that we are not distracted by anything or anyone, but fully immersed in the present moment. There's a massive difference between keeping a seat warm and using up the oxygen in the room and being mindfully present and available in both a physical and an emotional or a mental sense. Presence means that we are not thinking about what we are going to say next when the other person is done speaking. Presence means that we recognize that the future is only controlled by the present and the past is the result of what happens in the present, so neither the past nor the future is worthy of sacrificing presence in moments that require our attention.

Intention implies that we are not centered in the moment solely because we *have* to be in the moment, nor have we been forcibly placed into the moment by some irresistible force. For example, our attention is not present-centered only because a teacher or a parent has loudly demanded we pay attention, nor has our attention been snagged by some marvelous event, like an amazing sunrise or fantastic, irresistible event taking place in front of us. Rather than having some external force demand our attention, we become present-centered and aware by deliberate choice.

Noticing that which is new in the moment implies a certain curiosity about the intricacies of the moment and not allowing oneself to ignore details that may otherwise be considered mundane. This curiosity often arouses an appreciation for those details in addition to changing or altering one's perception of how those details combine to form the present moment.

Finally, and perhaps most difficult, one must be willing to adopt a general attitude of acceptance toward whatever arises in the present moment without judgment. When we allow ourselves to place judgments onto those occurrences, we become distracted and preoccupied by such judgments, removing our present-centered focus on the moment as a whole, as we ruminate on the value judgments we have placed on what we notice. Instead, if we accept those aspects of the moment as part and parcel with the moment itself, then we become more able to remain mindful of the moment as a whole.

The polar opposite of mindfulness is probably what you might expect it to be called—*mindlessness*. However, this is not intended to be a pejorative or insulting term. Mindlessness can be thought of as an inactive state of mind, the act of going through the motions, or being on autopilot and not thinking about what one is experiencing in the current moment. Contrary to what initial perceptions may arise when first considering this term, mindlessness is actually a necessary and imperative part of our lives. For example, if I am driving my car down the interstate at a speed of over 60 miles per hour, I should probably not suddenly become mindful of my surroundings by admiring the flora whizzing by outside the window, nor will I stop to mindfully and nonjudgmentally admire the craftsmanship of the stitching holding my car's interior together. If I did, then the next thing I would become mindful of is the guardrail, as my car bounces off of it—or worse. Mindlessness is necessary as a means to help us prioritize where we direct our attention. Another great example is with learning to ride a bike. Pedaling fast enough, adjusting the handlebars to keep the wheel straight, shifting our balance subtly from side to side—these are all elements of physics necessary for us to stay on two wheels, and yet, we can successfully ride a bike without having to consciously consider how we successfully achieve each of these items simultaneously. We do this by deprioritizing our attention on those items and, instead, allowing our bodies to take over where our mind leaves off. This way, we can redirect our attention to mindfully enjoy the scenery, the feel of the wind against our faces, and the physical exercise of riding a bike. Most of us probably do this automatically, and that is one of the key features of mindlessness.

Where mindfulness requires intentionality, mindlessness requires automatic and unintentional reactions, but these two intricately work together to help us direct our focus where it is most needed. The trouble comes into play when we switch between mindfulness and mindlessness, well, *mindlessly*.

Think of Doug, the happy-go-lucky dog from Pixar's *Up*, when his conversation is interrupted suddenly by—*SQUIRREL!* While this is a humorous example, it is only funny because it is most certainly a relatable example, as we currently live in a distraction-rich society, filled with seemingly endless opportunities for our attention spans to be yanked in several directions at once. As these distractions grow increasingly pervasive and effective, our collective ability to remain mindful, to select where we direct our attention, becomes critically important. Without mindfulness, we are little more than instinctive animals, snapping our gaze in the direction of whatever is loudest, shiniest, or most interesting. Like Doug, we may find ourselves failing to finish conversations with others because of a buzzing phone notification, or worse, we may find ourselves unable to finish a productive thought because of an advertisement.

I'd like to think that most of us do not want to see ourselves as a mindless product of social conditioning, and this book aims to bring control back to us as individuals, using mindfulness as the vehicle to arrive at our destination. Learning to become more mindful is something that can be achieved in as little as 10 minutes of committed effort each day, and mindfulness promises to:

- Increase awareness of one's surroundings, one's perceptions of events and people, and how others perceive us;
- Produce gratitude and a renewed sense of appreciation;
- Improve listening ability and increase empathic potential; and
- Deepen the quality of one's interpersonal relationships.

A little goes a long way toward becoming more mindful, so let's get started by diving into a quick warm-up exercise.

Activity #1: Turn It Off!

For this activity, you will attempt to stop thinking while you read the rest of the chapter. Your task is to simply focus on what you are reading, but any time—ANY TIME—you think of something other than what you are reading, even if it is related to the reading, make a hash mark in the margin of this book, even if you end up thinking about not thinking to avoid thinking or thinking about how your last hash mark looked. There is no measure of success with this exercise, but do not read any further until you have a pen or pencil, and you are ready to start marking. In fact, you may have already needed to mark at least a few hash marks since this paragraph began, but I haven't told you to start yet. Ready? Go!

Revolutions in Communication

To study human interaction is to recognize the tremendous impact that revolutions in the tools with which we communicate have made upon us as a species. To date, there have been four major revolutions in the way humans communicate, all four of which have been kicked off by the development and adoption of a new form of communication technology, with each shifting our messages from one preferred form to another.

Stop thinking about avoiding hash marks.

The first revolution was with the invention of written communication, at which point humans moved from being a primarily oral culture to a society that depended upon written communication. This happened several thousand years ago, and dates of this revolution vary greatly depending on where in the world we look, since the cultures all over the globe were not yet connected and able to share the discovery.

Are you being honest with yourself and marking EVERY time you think of something other than the reading?

The second revolution occurred at a precise time, in the middle of the 15th century, when Johannes Gutenberg invented moveable type for the printing press. Now, the press was already in existence, but Gutenberg's revolutionary idea (which seems so simple to us today) was to create individual letters that could be rearranged to print multiple documents using the same machine. This invention made printing significantly more efficient, which also reduced cost and increased availability. As a result, literacy began to rise, and common people started realizing that the church and other organizations, such as royalty and government, were taking advantage of them, and next thing we know, revolution broke out as we shifted from a leisure-reading culture to one that devoured information as it was produced at a much higher rate.

It's like telling you to not think of a pink elephant. Now, all you want to think about are pink elephants, right? Got you ... make a hash mark! Or don't, since technically, that pink elephant was part of the reading, right?

This radical increase in the sharing of information caused rapid advances in science, with respect to both the hard sciences, such as biology, physics, and chemistry, and social sciences, such as political science, sociology, and psychology. This led directly to the Industrial Revolution, as more available information sharing created giant leaps forward in improving and inventing new communication tools such as the camera, radio, television, and even the computer. Society shifted again, this time away from merely readers of information to interactive, individual consumer-producers, as people were able to express themselves with greater efficiency, rather than being limited to only consuming whatever was produced by larger organizations.

The Information Age

While the Internet was originally created as a U.S. Defense Department project in the mid-1970s, the release of the Internet to the general public in 1991 kicked off our most recent revolution, which has been dubbed by some, "The Information Age." It is characterized by the convergence of multiple forms of technology, but it is most evident in the widespread availability of information, as well as the ease with which information is created and shared.

> *It has often been said that seeking information via the Internet is like trying to take a drink from a fire hose!*

While perusing online articles in an attempt to make sense out of the scope of information currently being created, the term *zettabyte* became a new part of our collective vocabulary, and this is a 1 followed by 21 zeroes! A zettabyte was the amount of information projected for all of humanity to create during the year 2010. Compare this to the amount of information created by the culmination of humanity previously, calculated by an IBM supercomputer to be five *exabytes* (Rieland, 2012), which is a paltry 1/1000th of a zettabyte. While a statistical debate  currently rages as to the accuracy of these numbers, a core truth remains evident. Thanks in part to the vast array and ever-growing repertoire of tools available for creating and sharing information, we, as a species, have entered the Information Age, which may be viewed by future societies as a turning point for the human race. With radical change, however, comes a natural human tendency toward anxiety. When this natural fear is combined with feeling overwhelmed by the ever-present onslaught of information—some useful, but mostly not—one begins to see that the Information Age is not without its hazards. It might be tempting to subscribe to the notion of the sky succumbing to gravitational forces, had such a scenario not been without historical precedent, as we have seen in our glance at the history of communication technology.

Richard Saul Wurman (1989) famously proposed that, "A weekday edition of The New York Times contains more information than the average person was likely to come across in a lifetime in seventeenth-century England" (p. 32). Furthermore, he suggested that, for one to be a successful member of modern society, one must "assimilate a body of knowledge that is expanding by the minute" (p. 32). Taking into account that this was written two full years before the official release of the Internet to the general public, his proposition becomes more salient now than ever.

Still making hash marks in the margins? Or, have you started drawing pink elephants?

You might notice that, in reviewing this brief history of human communication, the period of time between revolutions has exponentially reduced with each successive revolution, from thousands of years between the alphabet and the printing press to hundreds of years between Gutenberg and the Industrial Revolution, so it's no surprise that we saw only decades pass between the tail end of the Industrial Revolution and the beginning of the fourth revolution: the Information Age, which I like to call the "Age of Distraction." We are currently in the midst of this revolution, kicked off by the advent of the Internet, and supercharged by the convergence of our immense networks with advances in mobile technology. We humans, with our innate need to be social, have learned to feed that craving by way of using mobile devices to effectively "plug in" to a global network of other humans. Society has moved away from the individual consumer-producer model to one where we are now primarily producers and sharers of information. Propagation of information is now effectively what we do best and most often.

As information becomes easier to create and share with others through an increasingly networked society, the dissemination characteristics of information have altered the behaviors of certain types of organizations. Industries such as journalism, book publishing, filmmaking, and music producing were once the prerogative of the well-networked or well-funded. In the past, to get a book published, an author had to write the tome, to polish it to perfection, and to spend months, if not years, querying agents and publishers in hopes that someone would find it worthy of elevation to the status of "published." Similarly, with music producing, artists would often play free shows with the hopes of being "discovered" by talent agents who may occasionally descend from their ivory towers to offer recording contracts. The Information Age, however, has turned these industries inside out and upside down. Anyone with a desire, a computer, and an Internet connection can publish a book or an article and can produce and distribute music or film. As a result, the information marketplace has become flooded to the point of supersaturation with information in various media. New organizations arise to fill the role of information curators, which are organizations whose sole purpose is to sift through the tide of new production, extract the best of the moment, and present it for us to consume. Think of these organizations as "filters" or "data miners" whose role is to find the best of the best and present that to us, tailored to our liking. However, the deluge of emerging information often sacrifices quality for timeliness in an attempt to be first, rather than the best, evident in the changing nature of journalism and the 24-hour news cycle. As our technological infrastructure becomes more efficient at the creation and distribution of new information, this trend will likely continue.

Because of this growing trend, the Age of Distraction has transformed the information marketplace from one that purports to sell media tailored to consumers' needs into one that simply competes for attention. The Age of Distraction has not made getting our drink from the proverbial fire hose easier; it has simply presented more fire hoses from which to choose. As a result, the information marketplace is now being run as an *attention economy* (Davenport & Beck, 2001). Herbert Simon (1971), writing from the brief gap between the Industrial Revolution and the Information Age, stated the following:

> ... in an information-rich world, the wealth of information means a dearth of something else: a scarcity of whatever it is that information consumes. What information consumes is rather obvious: it consumes the attention of its recipients. Hence a wealth of information creates a poverty of attention and a need to allocate that attention efficiently among the overabundance of information sources that might consume it. (pp. 40–41)

As our attention spans are increasingly taxed, becoming more fragile with each passing day, organizations operating within an attention economy will need to compete more ruthlessly for our attention as potential consumers, a complication of which we feel via unique anxieties, as our attention spans end up being pulled in several simultaneous, yet opposing directions.

The Age of Distraction also tends to make it harder for us to shut down, to where you aren't making so many hash marks in the margins. Blame it on your environment.

The Future of Communication

Merkushev Vasiliy/Shutterstock.com

Now, our question, as members of the society in which this revolution is upheaving, is as follows: What will the future hold for communication, and what will the next big revolution be? That is a question yet to be answered, though there are many theories. Perhaps the next leap forward will be in the communication of emotion, as our limbic brain (the ancient, more animalistic part of our brain responsible for the way we *feel*) has no capacity for language. Will future technology allow us to sense and translate emotions from human to human without the need for language, allowing us to empathize with one another more efficiently? Or, perhaps the next big advance will be along the lines of telepathy, allowing us to transmit thought without the need for language.

Regardless of what the future may hold, we live in an exciting time of flux and dynamic change. There are vast oceans of information at our fingertips, bringing with them myriad possibilities, but also potential for disaster. In the 1930s, at Harvard University, famed Psychologist B. F. Skinner developed what most of us call a "Skinner Box" but is more formally known as an operant conditioning chamber. In this now-famous experiment, Skinner initially placed a rat into a box with a lever inside. Whenever the rat pushed on the lever, a pellet of food would drop into the box. Initially, Skinner assumed that the rat would be unable to control itself and resort to gluttony, but much to his surprise, the rat exhibited self-control as it eventually learned the lever system and could predict the results. Skinner then modified the lever system to randomize the food pellet drop, and it was at this point that the rat became seemingly obsessed with the operation of the lever and ate far more food than before, when the results were predictable.

Why does this sound so familiar? People like us are conditioned like this every day. What do you do when your phone vibrates in your pocket? How about when you are working on something productive, but then you hear the familiar chime of a social media notification or a new e-mail?

Such are the levers of our society's proverbial Skinner Box, convincing us to mindlessly drop our attention and divert it to produce a conditioned response. The more so-called levers we utilize, the more distractions we must learn to live with, which also means the more distractions we must learn to resist if we want to become more mindful. Unfortunately, just as seeking information can feel like drinking from a fire hose, being mindful in the Age of Distraction can feel like swimming against a raging, torrential undertow.

To navigate the seas of information overload, we must take a step back and observe the changes and their effects upon the nature of interaction from a more mindful, objective perspective, rather than allowing ourselves to be caught up like rats in a Skinner Box, mindlessly clicking away on links generated by an algorithm that knows our deepest secrets. As with the alphabet, the printing press, and the Industrial Revolution, we will eventually grow accustomed to recent changes in due time, but only if we chart a careful, rational course. There are destined to be winners and losers emerging from the dust, as it settles, so which side will you be on? This is the impetus for our journey through the complexities of human communication, and this is our call to action to act mindfully as we work through these changes.

Those Hash Marks Though

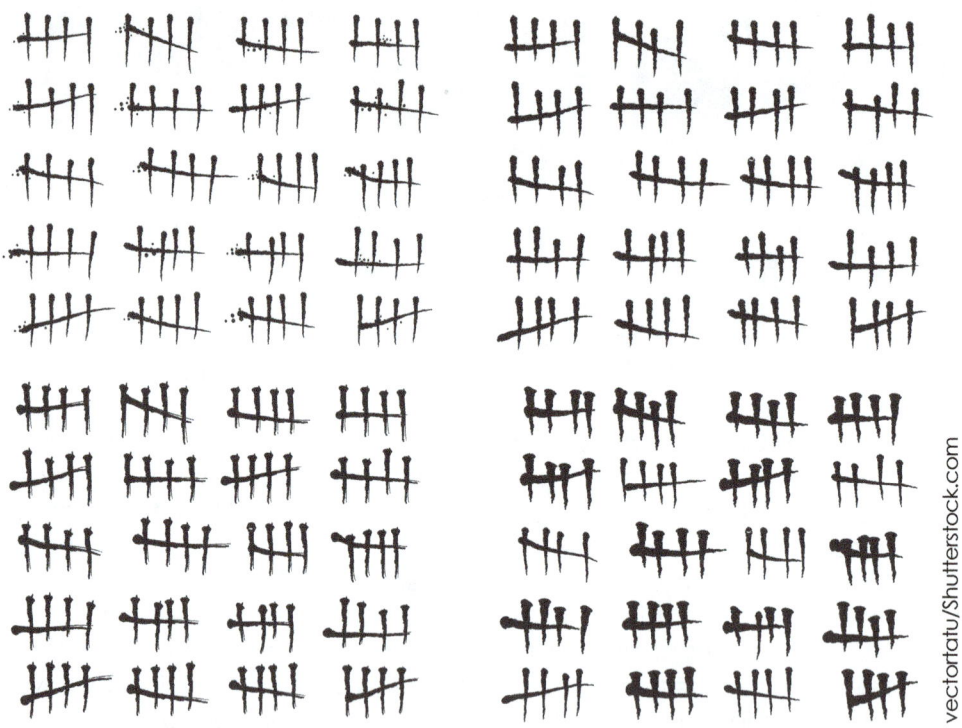

How did it go? Was it distracting to try to remain focused on the material, or did it get easier as you went through the passage? How much of the material did you actually retain? You may wish to go back and reread without doing the activity now to see how much you really remembered and how much that distraction affected your ability to retain information. This is what it's like living in the Age of Distraction. Our new communication media have turned us all into Doug, the dog, and we are, in a very literal sense, surrounded by proverbial squirrels at any given moment. This is why learning to be more mindful communicators is of such critical importance. However, this takes time and committed practice.

As we work through the rest of this book, we will work toward a goal of increasing our mindful behaviors. We will start with the prospect of becoming more self-aware in the first part of the book (Chapters 1–4), and then, in the second part (Chapters 5–8), we will examine the barriers that get in the way of mindful communication, such as anger, pride, ego, and poor listening habits. The third part of the book (Chapters 9–12) looks at how the field of positive psychology can help us all get more out of life using mindfulness as a vehicle, while the final part of the book (Chapters 13+) looks at how to utilize mindfulness to develop sustainable mindful interactions with the people most important to us.

For now, though, reflect on the following questions to test your understanding of the concepts in this first chapter:

- After completing this first activity, what implications does this have for your understanding of how much your thoughts control you, rather than the other way around?
- What effect does your control over intrapersonal communication have on your outward interactions?
- Cultures all over the world, since the beginning of time, have advocated the need for quiet self-reflection, meditation, or introspectively retreating into oneself to "recharge the batteries," so to speak. Some cultures have taken it to a religious level, associating it with prayer or communing with God, while others have linked it to rites of passage or the pursuit of wisdom. Why do you think we need to find ways to control our intrapersonal communication, and what role does mindful self-reflection play in this act?

References

Davenport, T. H. & Beck, J. C. (2001). *The attention economy: Understanding the new currency of business*. Cambridge, MA: Harvard Business Review.

Rieland, R. (2012, May 7). Big data or too much information? *Smithsonian*. Retrieved from http://www.smithsonianmag.com/innovation/big-data-or-too-much-information-82491666.

Wurman, R. S. (1989). *Information anxiety*. New York, NY: Doubleday.

CHAPTER 2

Paying Attention with Purpose

> People usually consider walking on water or in thin air a miracle. But I think the real miracle is not to walk either on water or in thin air, but to walk on earth. Every day, we are engaged in a miracle which we don't even recognize: a blue sky, white clouds, green leaves, the black, curious eyes of a child—our own two eyes. All is a miracle.
>
> —Thich Nhat Hanh

In the first chapter, we defined the concept of mindfulness and discussed what it means to be mindfully present versus simply taking up space in a physical sense. In this chapter, we will experiment with mindfulness-building activities to *see* and *feel* the impact mindfulness can have on our daily lives. These activities are not terribly difficult, nor are they time-consuming. In fact, most, if not all of these activities, can easily be incorporated into our daily routines with little to no adjustment in how we normally spend our time. The payoff to committing to them on a daily basis, however, is tremendous.

Before we get into the activities themselves, however, I need to provide some background and context to the exercises themselves, because each exercise arose out of a need for me to become more mindful in some way. I freely admit that I was not always mindful; in fact, I often related more to the concept of mindlessness than to mindfulness, and to this day, I still struggle to choose mindful presence over mindless distraction.

My journey toward mindfulness started in 2008, when I attended a weekend retreat at a monastery in Escondido, California, where I had the distinct pleasure of meeting Thich Nhat Hanh, the world-renowned Buddhist monk whose words grace the opening to this chapter. Shortly before learning about this retreat, I read of Hanh's influence on Martin Luther King, Jr., and how, after a meeting with Hanh, King became even more inspired to pursue his nonviolent protest movement that continues to inspire millions even today, more than half a century later. Knowing that such an influential figure was still around, I jumped at the opportunity. As Hanh spoke at the retreat, it felt like I was talking with an old friend I'd known my entire life. He had a way of speaking so conversationally, with such effortless ease, that everyone in his presence immediately felt as though Hanh's words had been chiseled out of the most valuable gemstones and given directly to them as a unique, one-of-a-kind gift. I remember walking away from that retreat thinking to myself, *I want to become mindful like Thich Nhat Hanh and in doing so, make those around me feel the kind of value that I just felt*. I knew that if I achieved only a mere fraction of what Hanh achieved throughout his life, then my interpersonal relationships would be deeper, more meaningful, and far more rewarding, not just for myself, but for everyone in my life. From that moment forward, I began to experiment with various mindfulness-building tools. Not all of them worked. In fact, some were abject failures, the sort of which I think I'll leave out of this book. The successes, however, I am happy to share.

Walks to Nowhere

I remember the day clearly. It was mid-summer, roughly at the point in the summer break where my kids and I start grinding on my wife's every last nerve. Being home during the summer requires a delicate balance between time spent with the family and alone time, but when that system goes out of balance, everyone grows irritable with one another. The irritability in question on this particular day resulted in a pretty heated argument, though I cannot remember for the life of me what started it. The only thing about it that I remember was that it was a doozy of a fight, and as it reached its zenith, I felt compelled to leave the house and go walk it off, so to speak.

I grabbed my two youngest kids by their hands and told them we were going on a walk, and they were happy to oblige. As we walked down the driveway toward the street, my youngest son asked where we were going, to which I tersely replied, "I don't know. It doesn't matter." As I was preoccupied with the rumination of thoughts swirling around my head regarding the argument, I told my children that they had free reign over where we would walk, so I let them lead the way. As they led me down the street, I began noticing a set of peculiar differences in this walk as compared to others.

First, we were walking significantly slower than I would normally walk for leisure. Our pace was probably cut in half, if not more, and if anything, I would describe our rate as meandering more so than walking. We stopped frequently to look at bugs in the grass, hop over cracks in the sidewalk, watch squirrels traversing the power lines above, or ask questions about the meanings behind street names every time we came to an intersection and saw the signs. This drastically reduced rate of speed also caused our peripheral field of vision to expand. The faster one moves, the greater the reduction in our peripheral view, and when driving at highway speeds, that reduction can be up to 75%. Suddenly, I was noticing more details in my neighborhood. I noticed my neighbors out working in their yards, and because I was walking by so slowly, it forced me to greet them and engage in small talk.

Second, I noticed how liberating it felt to relinquish control and decision-making to my children. By letting go of the idea of a destination, I had adopted an attitude of nonjudgmental acceptance, which was something I recalled Thich Nhat Hanh discussing when he suggested that, in mindful walking, we say to ourselves with every step, "I have arrived; I am home." I had nowhere to be and no time limit with which to arrive at such a destination. I was simply there with my kids, and nothing else mattered at that moment.

Eventually, my kids led me to a small park, and as we walked across the grass, I noticed a patch of clover, at which point I suggested that we lay down and try to find four-leaf clovers.

My children, being the wonderful, mindful beings that young children often are, did not hesitate to sit down and begin combing through hundreds of clovers leaves, searching for the ever-elusive lucky charm of a four-leaf clover. Call it fate if you will (or a disturbingly freak genetic anomaly), but within 15 minutes, we had found not just one, but four of the lucky clovers, which prompted a creative thought. I decided that we would gently bring them back home and try to preserve them by mounting them in clear epoxy, thereby creating a treasured memory.

When we got home, I cut up a cardboard tube from an empty toilet paper roll into small, one-inch sections as my form. I then laid down a layer of clear epoxy, placed the clover gently into the still-wet epoxy, and then laid down another layer. In less than 30 minutes, we cemented our lucky clovers in permanent fixtures, one of which I presented to my wife as a peace offering. To this day, neither my wife nor myself remember the source of the argument that kicked off the events of that day, but we all remember the good that arose from it, and none of it would have happened without our taking a walk to nowhere.

Last Supper

My wife and I were preparing a Szechuan stir fry for dinner, and I asked my oldest daughter, who happened to be a teenager at the time, if she knew where rice was harvested. As expected, she wagered a guess as to saying "Asia," which prompted me to help her do a little extracurricular homework before we ate. I pulled up a seat and popped open the laptop, and together, she and I perused pictures of rice fields and the people who work them. We watched a YouTube clip of how rice is harvested by hand and what workers' conditions are like. We then discussed what it takes

to get from harvesting to the table, from the people cleaning and packaging it, to the shipping workers loading it onto a boat and unloading it onto a truck, from the delivery driver who trucks it across the country, to the minimum-wage earning stock person working graveyard shift at the grocery store who placed it on the shelf for us to buy. And that was just the rice.

We then pondered what kind of process the green and red bell peppers went through, as well as the mushrooms, the baby corn, and the snow peas. By the time dinner arrived, all my daughter could do was stare at the plate in front of her. As she paused, I asked her what was wrong, and she told me that she was simply in awe of the network of human effort that went into producing this one meal in front of her at that moment. Eventually, she began eating, but as she ate, she took small bites and chewed them with intention. She savored every last delicate note of flavor and left nothing on her plate by the time she was done. Oddly, as she ate, my daughter had the most curious half-grin on her face, as though this meal was among the best meals she'd ever eaten. By slowing down and being deliberately intentional, all while absorbing the novelty of imagining the many hands that her food had passed through on its way to her plate, my daughter engaged in mindful eating, placing herself into a state of mindful presence.

Another way of doing this activity is to imagine that one's next meal is the last meal of one's life. Without getting overly melodramatic, using the imagination like this and pondering the what-ifs activate mindfulness in such a way as to allow for maximum appreciation of the food, as well as slowing down and truly noticing the many subtleties present. Rather than merely eating for the purpose of feeling full, such an activity allows us to savor our food and enjoy the miracle of the moment of the meal. Even if that meal is a cheap package of chicken ramen, one can still learn to fully savor and appreciate memories that may go hand in hand with such a meal. Personally, grilled cheese sandwiches do that for me, as I pretty much survived on grilled cheese growing up. Even though few would consider a grilled cheese sandwich a delicacy, and there isn't much of a flavor profile other than bread, butter, and cheese on the most basic version of the sandwich, the memories alone that such a meal invokes are worthy of absorbing myself into the moment of consumption. Slowing down, being deliberate and intentional, and allowing ourselves enjoyment of what we consume is a great mindfulness-building activity.

Red Light, Green Light

When I drive, I typically like to get in my car and head straight to the destination without having to stop. The only exception to that rule is when I am going on vacation and intentionally trying to enjoy the road trip, but even then, having to stop at red lights can get pretty annoying and ultimately, if I let it, becomes stressful. It's the idea that my forward progress to my goal is being impeded by this automated light system every few blocks or so, and the later I am in my normal schedule, the more stress arises because of my attachment to getting where I need to be on time.

Plyushkin / Shutterstock.com

As a result, I began employing a red light exercise I first heard during one of Thich Nhat Hanh's podcasts. In this talk, he brought up the very same stress I described above and, in doing so, described me perfectly. He then suggested that we consciously alter our perception of the red light by challenging our previously held symbolic interpretation of the red light. Instead of interpreting the red light as a barrier or impediment, he suggested viewing the light as a momentary relief from the chore of driving, a moment to gather my thoughts, re-center my thinking, and take in my surroundings.

Immediately after trying it for the first time, I began looking around at others who were stopped at the same light beside me. Some were singing. Others were dancing. Still more were picking their noses. Regardless of what the other drivers did, one thing was consistent: none of them noticed me watching them. So, I started making up stories about them. The lady in the white baseball cap just dropped her kids off and was on her way to tennis lesson with Serena Williams. The guy in the giant truck who I could barely see was a bronco busting cowboy on his way home from work on the ranch. All of a sudden, I began looking forward to the next red light because I had changed my perception of what it meant for me to be stopped for a minute or so. I began relaxing, breathing deeply, and smiling as my imagination took over. I still arrived at my destination on time, but significantly less stressed and more prepared for my daily interactions with others.

Hold the Phone

If you recall, in Chapter 1, I discussed the concept of a Skinner Box and operant conditioning, which causes us to engage in nearly obsessive behavior and based on that behavior somehow activating our brain's complex chemical reward system. Skinner's rat pushed the food lever repeatedly once the lever was fixed such that it rewarded the rat randomly instead of predictably. We humans are also animals and possess the same basic concept of a reward system in our brains. That stated, consider how we humans crave social interaction. In fact, a lack of social interaction, according to a recent study (Holt-Lunstad, Smith, & Layton, 2010), social isolation has a comparable mortality rate to smoking! Ultimately, loneliness can eventually kill you. Think about the implication of that. Seeking out others and being social is a survival mechanism built into our DNA. Therefore, it should come as no surprise that the reward centers in our brains are activated by positive social interactions. Now, combine this new knowledge with the tools we currently have available to us to connect with one another socially. Skinner's concepts are easily seen in how we react to a brief vibration or custom ringtone that goes off whenever we get a new text message, e-mail, social media notification, or phone call. How much time elapses between the moment you hear or feel that notification and the moment you check your device or computer? If you're anything like the rest of humanity, I'd wager not a lot. Most of us become so easily conditioned to check our notifications that we begin to easily resemble Doug from the movie *Up*, only our irresistible squirrel is an electronic device of some kind letting us know that someone out there chose us for interaction.

As an alternative to that conditioning, I used what I knew about the red-light activity to reframe my perception of these notifications. Instead of leaping immediately to check the notification and allowing them to control my reaction, I decided that the notifications were now going to be redefined as reminders to stop whatever I'm doing, take a few deep breaths, and then look at who is trying to contact me. Before reviewing their message or answering their phone call, I stop for a moment and ponder what that person is going through at that moment. If it's a number I don't recognize, I employ my imagination, similar to how I used it during the red-light activity.

Even if that person is a telemarketer from Sri Lanka, I stop to think about how many irate people that sadly underpaid call center employee has had to deal with before calling me. Eventually, I do have to answer the phone or read the text or e-mail, but I do so only after clearing my mind of distraction and allowing the other person to have the better part of my intentional, purposeful attention. Doing this, I notice, as with the other exercises, my stress level decreases, and I feel less of a sense of urgency to respond. I choose my response much more carefully and mindfully, returning control to me, rather than allowing systematic notifications control me.

So What?

Throughout this chapter, you've read stories of how I came to discover a love of mindfulness through diverse activities, each of which sharpens and focuses a specific facet of mindfulness:

- Going for a walk to nowhere allows us to develop a greater appreciation and awareness of our surroundings, while also exercising our ability to let go of the habit of always looking out for the next destination.
- Mindful eating teaches us to savor our food and slow down, which, by the way, is a proven way to end up eating smaller portions, since it takes about 20 minutes for signals from our stomachs to reach our brains, letting the brain know that our hunger has been satisfied. Eating slowly and deliberately also allows us to enjoy our meals more, but in addition, thinking about where our food comes from can give us a greater appreciation for it, as well as forcing us to think more critically about what we choose to eat.
- The red-light activity reduces stress and teaches us to intentionally reshape our perception of potentially annoying and/or stressful things in our daily lives, but it also engages the imagination and provides a bit of entertainment during an otherwise droll commute.
- Learning to pause before responding to a device notification returns to us a semblance of control, rather than allowing operant conditioning to take place, giving too much control to our devices. Moreover, that pause also allows us to place ourselves in the right frame of mind before engaging in interaction with others.

Now, it's your turn. Try each of these activities, preferably on separate days. Avoid trying them all at once, but instead, spread them out over time so that you get the full benefit and determine just how these activities can make a difference in your daily life. Fair warning, though, not all people will resonate with all the activities, so don't go into it expecting to reach enlightenment or achieve a suddenly profound awakening! What we are looking for are small, incremental, subtle changes, which, over time, result in profound reductions in stress, increases in appreciation, and, most importantly, a heightened sense of self-awareness.

Conversely, you can also choose to modify the activities. Ponder this: where do your best ideas seem to happen? For many, it happens while taking a shower, while sitting on the porcelain throne, or while doing some menial chore. What does each of these activities have in common? They are all painfully simple activities requiring a bare minimum of concentration, which allows us to quiet our minds and let the creativity flow through us. With that stated, another type of meditation like the aforementioned activities involves doing simple chores, such as the dishes, folding laundry, mowing the lawn, shoveling snow, and even cooking. Approach such a chore with a similar attitude to the red-light challenge, where you intentionally and deliberately change your mental approach. Accept the chore for what it is, but alter your perception of the chore. Think of it not as a chore, but as a service to others. Tap into your gratitude and appreciate that you are able to serve others in this way, and then lose yourself in the moment.

Regardless of which exercises you choose to do first, set yourself a goal to try each of the exercises from this chapter over the course of the next week, with the aim of doing one per day. As you do them, reflect on the following questions as food for thought:

- There is a big difference between going through the motions and operating on autopilot while interacting with others and truly being present, on purpose, with intention. What role does intentional, mindful presence have on communication in your life?
- Where have you witnessed it in others, and what impact did seeing others being present have on your perception of that person?
- What times have you noticed yourself doing it? How did it feel for you to lose yourself in the power of the moment?

Reference

Holt, L. J., Smith T. B., & Layton, J. B. (2010) Social relationships and mortality risk: A meta-analytic review. *PLoS Med* 7(7): e1000316. doi:10.1371/journal.pmed.1000316

CHAPTER 3

Perception of Self and Perceptions of Others

> There are things known, and there are things unknown, and in between are the doors of perception.
>
> —Aldous Huxley

Standing on the bottom step of a ramshackle porch outside my single-wide trailer, beer in one hand and cigarette in the other (side note: I quit smoking over a decade ago), our conversation rambled from one topic to any number of unrelated others. There we stood—me, along with my wife, and one of my good friends from college who was in town for a visit—getting together at my place for a debaucherously good weekend, which sounds much cooler than it really was. In reality, we simply networked our computers together to play first-person shooter games, drink the same cheap beer we did in college, and bond over the experience.

As the wind chill cut through the haze of smoke, I listened to my friend rattle off a story about what was happening back in the old college town, when suddenly, he stopped, mid-sentence, and said, "You know, Josh, I hate it when you do that."

My mind was shaken, and I was taken aback by his sudden critique. "Hate what, exactly? What did I do?"

"You do it all the time," he continued, "You checked out of the conversation, and now, you're thinking of the next thing you want to say, which is probably a story to top mine."

Shocked and bewildered, I persisted in my denial, "No I wasn't!"

"Yes, you were," he snapped back. "You get this glazed-over look in your eyes . . . happens all the time, man, and it drives me nuts!"

Still confused, I turned to my wife, hoping for her to come to my defense, only to be met with her nodding and a quick, "Yep, he's right. You do it all the time."

Thinking of a quick comeback, I fired off the only thing I could muster, "If I do it all the time, then why is this the first I'm hearing of it?"

My friend was the first to speak up, "Because whenever anyone criticizes you, you get obnoxiously defensive." He then compared my defensiveness to a particular bodily orifice. I'll let you guess which one.

Ouch, I thought to myself. His remark cut deep. Turning again to my wife, her head still nodding in agreement, she remarked, "Truth. You really are a jerk whenever anyone criticizes you."

For the remainder of the evening, their concerted attack on my identity was all I could think of. Had I really been like this all my life? If they knew, but didn't want to tell me, how many of my past relationships might have failed because of this quality? I decided that the next morning, I was going to find some answers, so I called the friend who had known me the longest, only to be met with the exact same reply, which was worded almost verbatim, including the referenced bodily orifice.

This newfound truth rocked me to my core, and not in a hyperbolic hipster sort of exaggeration that is so prevalent in today's social media clickbait headlines. I found myself suddenly and unexpectedly facing a side of me I never knew I had and wondering how many others in my past perceived me in this manner. From that point forward, I started paying more attention to the sound and tone of my words, particularly when being criticized, and sure enough, they were all right. Criticism was the catalyst that transformed me from Dr. Jekyll into Mr. Hyde and was it ever ugly and unbecoming.

What I had experienced in this tale was opening myself up to what is called the blind spot. In communication studies, we frequently reference the Johari Window. Named for its founders, *Joseph* Luft and *Harrington* Ingham, the Johari Window is a concept that suggests we have four areas of our identity: 1) a public self that is known to ourselves and others; 2) a private self that is known only to us; 3) an unknown self that is neither open to the public nor us; and 4) a "blind spot," which is what others know about us that we are not yet aware of ourselves.

	Known to Self	Unknown to Self
Known to Others	**Public Self**	**Blind Spot**
Unknown to Others	**Private Self**	**Unknown**

The Johari Window
Adapted from *Luft, J. & Ingham, H. (1955). "The Johari window, a graphic model of interpersonal awareness". Proceedings of the western training laboratory in group development. Los Angeles: UCLA.*

If we imagine the center point of this grid being flexible and able to move around the larger square, depending on our experiences and circumstances, we can see that, for some, the pane for the Public Self may larger (and consequently, the Private Self gets smaller) if that person exhibits a greater degree of self-disclosure. Conversely, the Public Self grows smaller if that person tends to be quieter and more reserved, while the Private Self grows larger in response. The right side of the grid—that which is unknown, whether to self or others—shrinks as a person develops a greater sense of self-awareness.

Particularly dangerous, however, is the pane for the Blind Spot. A blind spot, as in my case, could be the potential cause for many a failed relationship. For the better part of my young adult life, I could not, for the life of me, figure out why it seemed like I couldn't maintain longer term friendships, but once I learned about my ego-defensive tendencies, all became clear. A blind spot is also dangerous because of its power over our subconscious behaviors, to the point where, as the blind spot is discovered, it could present a serious threat to one's identity. If we are not flexible and resilient enough to face the impending change presented by learning of the blind spot, we may very well build up walls to keep others away.

Activity: Facing the Blind Spot

For this activity, I'm asking you to undertake a potentially difficult and uncomfortable assignment, but approach it with courage and trust that, in the end, it will pay off. It could end up being one of the hardest activities in this book to complete, but it is an absolutely necessary one. Ready? Here's the description of the activity (but don't do it yet):

> Contact a close friend, family member, mentor, or anyone else close to you who knows you very well, and invite this person to share a meal with you. During the meal, tell this person that you have something important to ask and that, once you have asked the question, you have been strictly instructed to listen carefully and not defend yourself in any way. Tell the person that nothing is off limits and that you are not allowed to respond defensively—only to listen with an open heart and mind. Encourage complete and even brutal honesty in this person's response to your question. Once this person clearly understands the conditions of responding, ask this person to share with you the one thing about you that annoys her or him most.

As you can imagine, this is a gut-wrenching and potentially life-altering exercise in self-awareness. First of all, the other person is someone important in our lives, so their opinion obviously matters a great deal, presenting a threat to our vulnerability. After all, what if the other person reveals something life-altering that we cannot ever unhear? How might we see ourselves differently after that moment, knowing that something potentially serious bugs one of these people who matter most to us?

Second, not being allowed to defend ourselves during the exercise opens up the other person to being more honest and forthright, but more importantly, it causes us to listen more deeply. Rather than listening so that we can gather information to use in our strategic defense of the ego, we must sit quietly and dwell on the information, looking at it in terms of the other person, which is the core of empathic listening.

In all the years in which I have employed this exercise, I have heard a wide array of responses reported from those who have taken part in it, but to date, I have never once heard someone come back from the activity with anything but a profound learning experience. Allowing others to shine a light on our blind spots, particularly with respect to our faults, teaches us how to become better conversationalists, better listeners, and, ultimately, better people in general. What we learn about our blind spots may not always be pleasant, but it can open up a whole new world we never even knew existed.

In addition to the content of the response, we might be able to read into the way in which the response was given. Sometimes, what we hear may simply confirm something we already knew existed, but it may be presented to us in a way that underlines the extent to which it gets under the other person's skin. Often times, we might have annoying habits, but the people around us might be too polite, too anxious, or too downright scared to share that extent with us, for whatever reason. Sometimes, the other person might need to think for a while about the response, which also tells us something. Either there could be a plethora of responses from which to choose, or more likely than not, it could be that the other person is having a difficult time thinking of something with which to respond. On the other end of that spectrum, the other person may have an immediate response, to the point where the quickness with which they respond presents us with the realization that this is something that has been in the forefront of the other person's mind. Then, the question becomes, why haven't they said something sooner?

In all the years I've employed this exercise, I also partake in it, because I would never ask students to do something I wouldn't be willing to do myself, which means that I've done this exercise at least three times a year for the better part of a decade. Trust me when I state categorically that this exercise produces better results if undertaken regularly. I generally ask my family and close friends, with an occasional coworker thrown in for good measure, but one time, I asked my two youngest children the question on the drive home from school. They both hesitated at first, but then they spoke openly and comfortably with me:

From my 7-year-old son: "It makes me sad when you yell at me, Dad. It makes me feel like you don't love me anymore, and it makes me want to go hide in my room."

From my 10-year-old daughter: "I don't like it when you get mad at me, either. It hurts me and makes me cry. I don't want to make you mad."

At that point, I could no longer concentrate on the road, so I pulled over, and on the side of road, I unbuckled my seat belt so that I could hug them both, embracing them tightly. Swept up by a moment of pure clarity and raw openness, we all shed a few tears in an embrace that felt like an eternity.

Slowly, as we calmed down, I pulled away from our group hug so that I could see their faces. Wiping my eyes and theirs, I said, "I'm sorry. I didn't realize I had been yelling so much lately, and even though I get frustrated with you two at times, I don't want you thinking I'm mad at you. I promise that I will do better."

I could have told them that my yelling had a purpose. I could have brought up all the fights they had, all the times they forgot their chores, all the things they've broken, and any of the other plethora of mistakes they've made. But I didn't. Instead, I gave them their moment to vent. Instead, I gave them the gift of listening without judgment. I did this in an effort to teach my children humility by example, to show them that it is possible to hear others' critique, absorb it, and then actually do something to change that which necessitates change out of a spirit moved by love. Mainly, I did it because, as with the first time I confronted the demon in my blind spot, standing outside a single-wide trailer all those years ago, it wasn't so much that I cared about what others thought of me, but how I saw myself reflected back.

Our identities are formed throughout a complex web of interaction. Part of how we come to see ourselves lies in how others see us as well, but those don't always align perfectly. This is what is known as the *looking glass self*. Basically, this concept states that we shape our self-concepts based on our understanding of how others perceive us. Wrap your mind around that for a second. The image of ourselves that we regularly imagine is essentially a mixture of how we see ourselves combined with how we imagine others see us, a perception of others' perceptions, if you will. What this means for our understanding of this exercise is that, when faced with a challenge to that set of perceptions, it can radically redefine how we see ourselves.

It's no wonder why the exercise is so awkward, and it's no mystery why we feel so much anxiety heading into the exercise. If that much of our self-perceptions are tied up in how others see us, and if any uncertainty exists in regard to how we think others might respond, then the sensation evoked by this mixture of emotion is simply this: vulnerability.

One of the most nerve-wracking times I ever did this exercise was, believe it or not, on one of my colleagues. It was the first time I had ever even considered asking one of my peers, and the anxiety I felt heading into our conversation was noticeably higher than it was with either my wife or my children, but why? Simply put, when I'm at home with my family, I am a father or husband, where I am considerably more comfortable and at ease with that identity. When I go to work, I am an educator, which is an identity fraught with uncertainty. My relative comfort in the identity of educator is reasonably comfortable, but I still felt the sting of vulnerability as I asked my colleague to tell me what about me bugged her the most. Questions flooded my mind as I asked her:

- What if the old arrogant jerk thing comes up with her like it did before, with my wife and college friend?
- What if I haven't improved at work like I have at home?
- What if she tells me that I need to improve on listening to others at work?
- What if I learn about some new, unknown behavior, like "mansplaining" to women at work or constantly interrupting others?

In other words, what if the way I saw myself before asking her was way off base and it turned out that I had considerable work to do? Such a realization may be painful and temporarily demoralizing, but in the long run, beneficial, for when I take such criticism to heart as a way to find out what to work on with respect to my relationships, then my relationships will develop, grow, and, ultimately, flourish. Each time I conduct this exercise (and I have repeated it often with those whom I care about the most), I consider the following: I am slowly chipping away at my ego and using the proverbial pieces that are chipped off as a material with which to build stronger, more resilient bridges in my relationships with people I care about the most.

Fortunately for me (and my fragile ego), her response, though unexpected, was far from life-altering. If anything, it pointed to something I should be keeping a closer eye on with respect to how I divvy up my time among various projects. After her response, I felt the all-too-familiar weights being lifted off my chest, realizing that the way I saw myself was reasonably congruent with the way at least one of my colleagues saw me, so until next time, when I choose a new colleague to ask, I feel more at ease.

Now, it's your turn to conduct the exercise as described. Choose someone you care about, and it should be someone who knows you pretty well. Invite that person to sit down to share a meal with you (preferably a good one). Explain to that person that you have something important to discuss and that, in a moment, you will ask her or him a question. Tell your dining partner that, once the question is asked, you cannot defend yourself, but only listen deeply and ask clarifying questions if needed. Encourage the person to be brutally honest if need be, and ensure the person feels comfortable responding. Then, however you wish to phrase the question, ask the other person to describe the one thing about you that bugs/annoys/drives her or him nuts the most. As the other person responds, pay close attention to the feelings that arise in you. Do you feel a slight twinge of defensiveness? Do your shoulders tense up or do your ears or cheeks begin to feel warm? Notice how it feels to become defensive, and allow those feelings to pass without heeding them. Let go of those urges and, instead, focus solely on understanding the other person.

Then, soon after your conversation, fill out the form on the next page. Include as much detail as possible, and once you are finished, follow the instructions on the bottom of the page.

Checking the Blind Spot

Use the space below to write down—in detail—what bugged someone else most about you, as divulged from the person (or people, if you were brave enough to do it more than once) you chose to ask this activity. Speculate on why you might do this and where it may have originated. Imagine how you might feel if someone close to you did this same behavior to you. Once finished, follow the instructions at the bottom of the page.

_____
_____
_____
_____
_____
_____
_____
_____
_____
_____
_____
_____
_____
_____
_____
_____
_____
_____
_____
_____
_____
_____
_____
_____
_____

Finished? Good.

Tear out this page and creatively destroy it. Ideas include the following: burning it, running over it with your car, blacking out the page with a permanent marker, running it through a garbage disposal, making confetti out of it using a chain saw, using it for target practice, all of the above, and so on. Regardless of how you destroy it, as you eliminate this page from existence, imagine yourself destroying not only a piece of paper, but a negative behavior that drives a wedge between you and someone you care about. As you destroy the page, commit to resolving the behavior and strengthening your relationship.

CHAPTER 4

Learning to Be Alone

> I love to be alone. I never found the companion that was so companionable as solitude.
> —Henry David Thoreau

One certainty we all generally experience while living in the Age of Distraction is that we are rarely ever more than a click away from connecting with someone else, from interacting with other people, or from busying our minds with a form of entertainment, education, or some other form of stimulus. But how often are we ever alone—truly and completely alone? How often do we take a significant chunk of time out of our days to intentionally and willfully be alone and do nothing other than to be alone with our thoughts? To illustrate the importance of being alone and doing nothing, allow me to share yet another story from my life experience . . .

After graduating with my bachelor's degree in applied communication studies, I knew I had to get a "real" job—you know, just one job with a relatively decent paycheck that not only made me feel like my tuition money for the last four years had been worth the journey, but one that also supported my family better than the three simultaneous part-time jobs I had during school, including pizza delivery, cleaning dog kennels at the Humane Society, and cleaning toilets. Luckily, I ended up with a reasonably lucrative human resource executive position for a large retail company, but the downside to it was that I was expected to work upwards of 50 hours per week. Combine my work schedule with grad school, where I was expected to read six to ten books per eight-week course and write nearly ten pages of academic work each week, and the recipe for stress begins taking shape. If that wasn't enough, I was also a husband and a father of four children, one of whom was a newborn baby boy at the time.

At some point during the first year or so of grad school, I settled into a routine, but my routine had no room for error, such as sickness (whether for me or my family) or other calamity, so to state that my schedule was as fragile as blown sugar is an understatement. Still, I managed to keep it all together, that is, until I got the phone call of a lifetime. Right before my final semester before earning my master's degree (note: my final semester would entail conducting a research study and writing a subsequent thesis, along with four other classes during a five-month period), I received a surprise phone call from the division chair of the college for which I wished to teach, inviting me to come teach a class or two part-time for them. The division chair told me that she had heard I was nearing the end of grad school, and since I was not only an alum of the college, but also had built strong relationships with the faculty there, she wanted to invite me to get some experience under my belt. Stunned, I accepted her offer without even considering how it might affect me or my family. I knew enough about the career field of teaching in higher education to know that, if I wanted a full-time, tenure-track position in communication, then I would typically have to wait for someone to either die or retire, because positions simply don't open up that often. So, I shot one from the proverbial hip, accepted the offer, and figured I would come up with a solution later.

That's when the real stress hit. Almost immediately, I showed all the symptoms of pre-burnout and high stress: irritability, chronic fatigue, forgetfulness, high anxiety, mild depression, and so on. While I had found a way to sneak in this new opportunity, I was not only burning the candle at both ends—I had incinerated the whole candle in a brilliant, fiery inferno, and I was watching it slowly fade away! My wife, in all her brilliance and wisdom, noticed the change in my behavior and mood, and she pulled me aside. In her classic not-so-gentle, yet somewhat blunt and direct way (see the story in the previous chapter regarding my blind spot), she told me that my behavior simply could not stand anymore and that I needed to do something about it—or else. Of course, in all my typical defensiveness, I became angry, sanctimonious, and self-righteous, but then it struck me—as usual, she was right. So, I asked what she would like for me to do, and the solution she came up with sounded absolutely clinically insane. She wanted me to go to work and teach classes as normal, but when I got home at the end of the day, I would devote all my time and attention to her and the children until the kids went to bed (which was typically around 8:00 p.m. or so). From the kids' bedtime forward, I had that time to concentrate on my schoolwork, and we would stick to that routine six days a week, with Saturday being the only exception. She demanded that my Saturdays (when I wasn't working of course, since I did work for a retail company) be not only devoted to family, but also technology-free.

I honestly did not know how to take her demands. I thought she was nuts for even suggesting such a crazy schedule. To be frank, I was having trouble keeping my head above water with the schedule I did have, and yet, she wanted me to nearly halve my schoolwork time throughout the week by sacrificing it for family time. However, I trusted her completely and decided to give her suggestion a try. To make the most of my time, I made a to-do list and determined how many hours in each day of the week I would need to get done everything I needed to do. Then, as I did those items, I noticed something interesting—because of the to-do list and dedicated time, I found that I was not as scattered and disorganized. Suddenly, I was making the most out of the time I set aside for each item, and believe it or not, I was getting more done with less time.

The important part of this story is in how far ahead I got with my schedule that I quickly found an extra 15–20 minutes at the end of each day, and considering that it was late at night (or early morning, depending on how one might look at 1:00–2:00 a.m.), everyone else in the house was asleep, leaving me with complete peace and quiet. As a result, I decided to give myself that time each and every night, to unwind, to decompress, and to allow the weight of all my stress to dissipate before I went to bed. And you know what? I suddenly began sleeping much more efficiently as well! By turning off the computer, all the lights, and putting my phone away, leaving only me and my thoughts in the dark by myself for 15 minutes, it genuinely felt as though my stress melted away in that brief amount of time. By the moment I went to bed, I was generally asleep before my head even hit the pillow. In yoga, a similar technique is employed at the end of a yoga session and is called *Savasana* or *Mrtasana*, which translates to "corpse pose."

The pose is designed to allow practitioners of yoga to fully relax and recharge at the end of a strenuous session, and people will often describe falling asleep during this pose because of its effectiveness. What this yoga pose and my 15 minutes of nothingness have in common is that they both encourage being alone, spending time in mindful thought, and instead of tuning everything out, allowing thoughts to come and go like clouds passing through an otherwise blue sky, while I allow those thoughts to pass without latching on to any one thought.

The Importance of Being Alone and Doing Nothing

The practice of taking 15 minutes out of every day to be alone and do nothing taught me several things, but the most important lesson I learned was a greater appreciation of the present. During those nighttime "meditation" sessions, I was able to let go of the past, whether I was dwelling on older things that kept swimming around in my head or recent events that I'd experienced earlier that day. I was also able to let go of the future and stop running through my to-do list and all that needed to get done later, since I was comfortable in knowing that I had already written it down, so there was no need to ruminate about it. Instead, as I let go of both the past and the future, I focused solely on the present, in which there was nothing—and it was gloriously relaxing.

If being immersed in the present and doing nothing is so fabulous, then why don't we allow ourselves a regular moment of nothingness while alone more frequently? One main reason for this inhibition or avoidance of being alone with nothing to do is due to life within the Age of Distraction. We become easily conditioned to always be busy or to always have something occupying our minds. You've probably seen the scenario pictured above. You may have even been one of those people on your device while someone was trying to talk with you. To view this behavior in the wild, simply go to a park with children's toys, and watch the parents. It is extremely likely that the majority of them are not necessarily watching their children, nor are they engaged in play with them. Most are likely craning their necks, looking down at a screen. It isn't solely parents, though; we see the same behavior everywhere—while waiting in the grocery store checkout line or the line to buy concert tickets; while taking breaks

at work; while walking just about anywhere; while shopping; in between periods or quarters at a sporting event—the list goes on and on. Just about any time that we are faced with the prospect of being alone and having nothing to do, we habitually reach for the phone. The alternative, of course, is to look around and take stock of our surroundings, to notice the intricacies of our environments, or to strike up a conversation with either a stranger or the people we know who are with us. This conditioned behavior is stabbing at the very fabric of
our social system, potentially threatening to cause us to forget how to interact with one another in person. Additionally, this creates what I call an *impatient space*. Try the impatient space activity just for fun and pay close attention to how quickly you begin to feel a sense of urgency or awkwardness. How quickly do you feel the urge to break the silence or reach for your phone?

> **IMPATIENT SPACE ACTIVITY.** *Find a willing partner or, for bonus points, a willing group, to help with this activity. Eliminate any outside distractions such as a television, radio, computers, or phones first, but you will need a timer of some sort. Set the timer for three minutes, and when you all are ready, be silent for the entire three-minute period. Pay close attention to the feelings that arise and at what point in the period they emerge. Also, pay attention to your nonverbal signals, along with your partner or group's nonverbal signals. What do they do with their eye contact? Do they show any visible nervous symptoms? Most of all, take note of the anxious feelings of impatience during this three-minute period.*

In addition to living in an impatient space, I would also argue that most of us are afraid of being alone because we busy ourselves and distract ourselves so much with other tasks and thoughts so that we don't have to be alone with our thoughts. I wager that many of us are downright afraid of what thoughts or feelings may come bubbling up to the surface. In fact, the more we busy ourselves and avoid being by ourselves, the higher the odds seem to be that there is something unpleasant that we have pushed down into the shadows and recesses of our subconscious, avoiding it, refusing to face it, and ultimately procrastinating the task of coping with that unpleasantness.

Being alone sometimes requires a touch of courage and trust in the process. It requires facing those thoughts, accepting them for what they are, and letting them pass. If those same thoughts continue to resurface, then we know that those are the thoughts that are contributing to our stress and anxiety, and perhaps, the issues causing those thoughts need to be dealt with more immediately.

It's like when we get a piece of popcorn stuck in between our teeth and have nothing to get it out. What happens? Every five seconds or so, we check on the tooth again to make sure it's still there. We obsess over it repeatedly until we can get it out! The same goes for our thoughts. We notice a thought that makes us feel anxious, and the next time it comes up, we feel even more anxious because we notice it again. Before we know it, we start feeling anxious about getting anxious because we know that the thought is going to appear again!

Speaking of ruminating on a single thought again and again, think back to perhaps a time when someone said something that offended you, and I'm not simply talking about something generally offensive, but something genuinely and personally offensive, as though it cut you deeply in the proverbial sense. How easy was it for you to let that go? Did you even let it go? Some of us might still be carrying around those moments. Ultimately, what happens is that we replay the event in question on repeat in our minds. Sometimes, we even start to run imaginary scripts of what we should have said or done in response. Other times, we might imagine a dialogue for whenever the situation presents itself again in the future. In the end, the other person whose message offended us ends up living in our heads for an extended period of time, rent-free.

When we sit down to do nothing, some of those situations might emerge as we try to clear our minds. As we notice those thoughts, it becomes exceedingly difficult to notice those thoughts and memories, and simply allow them to pass without latching on to them. This is usually because we have avoided facing those thoughts and coping with them, and this is our mind's way of pointing out to us that it's time to put up or shut up! The harder a thought is to let pass, the more important it becomes for us to face and deal with at some later time. Such is the importance of doing nothing. As we reduce our actionable state to zero, what remains in our minds as the dust settles is that which is important and pressing. Doing nothing is like shining a spotlight on our biggest unresolved issues, providing us with the guidance needed to know where we should begin.

Another analogy, as mentioned earlier, is that of clouds in the sky. If we pretend that blue skies represent a state of happiness, and clouds are the barriers that prevent us from achieving full happiness, then we can understand how, at times, that sky looks pretty well overcast, without a trace of blue to be found. In such scenarios, it is easy for us to forget about the blue sky that remains above the clouds that represent stress, anxiety, and/or despair. Since we tend to focus on what is right in front of us, and clouds are all we see, we assume that's all there is. However, by taking just 15 minutes out of our days to do nothing and pretend we are pulling up a chair outside to watch clouds go by, we can learn to let those thoughts pass without latching on to them. We notice them, acknowledge their existence, and allow them to continue on their way until  they no longer occupy the focal point of our minds. Eventually, our minds run out of clouds, and all that is left is the calm, serene, and, ultimately, contentment of a clear and relaxed state of mind. At that point, we are recharged and refreshed, ready to take on the issues pervading our worried states of mind.

Activity: Learning to be Alone

As you wrap up this chapter, set aside one hour in your week as soon as possible. Then, spend that hour alone in thoughtful reflection—absolutely no other people, no electronics, no reading books (though you'll want to bring this one with you, along with something to write with), no pets ... completely and utterly alone and without distraction. During this time, take notice of the thoughts that arise and practice treating those thoughts like passing clouds in an otherwise blue sky of your mind. Do this for at least 15 minutes as you begin your hour (no need to time it exactly—simply guess), and then, for the next 45 minutes, perform on yourself what is called a *communication audit*. A communication audit is basically what it sounds like; one at a time, you take inventory of your communication abilities within various facets of communication. To get you

started, here is a list that looks at communication from the inside out, from the simplest means of communication to the largest-scale mode of communication:

- Intrapersonal communication (how we communicate with ourselves, better known as *thought*);
- Nonverbal communication (ability to both control body language, appearance, use of personal space, and so on, as well as your ability to interpret nonverbal signals accurately);
- Interpersonal communication (proficiency with one-on-one interaction);
- Intercultural communication (how you interact with others from different backgrounds, such as people from a different ethnicity, nationality, religion, political preference, sexual orientation, gender, and socioeconomic class);
- Small group communication (how you interact with others in a group setting, such as work, school, or even family);
- Public speaking (being the focal point and delivering a message to a group);
- Mediated communication (texting, e-mail, social media, and so on); and
- Mass media (what you choose to consume and how frequently you consume mass media, such as television, music, literature, or online publications).

As you work your way through this list (which is partly why I suggested bringing this book along), reflect on your strengths as well as your areas for improvement in each area. The more detailed your audit, the more valuable this hour alone will eventually become to you later in the book. Additionally, give attention to how you feel and the emotional states you transition to and from during this hour of solitary reflection.

When the hour is up, use the space below to capture your initial thoughts and reflections. What thoughts came and went? Did any of them continue to return? How did this hour make you feel? Did you go through a wide range of emotional states, and if so, what were they? How comfortable were you being alone with nothing to do? Is this something you think would be beneficial to do on a regular basis? What areas of communication really stand out to you as providing opportunities for growth and development? In which areas do you feel strongest? Include reflections on all of these questions below, but leave some extra room. After you wake up the following morning immediately after doing this activity, jot down some notes about whether it was easier to sleep or not. If it was easier for you to fall asleep, or if you slept more deeply, what does this say about the need to unwind and be alone, doing nothing, on a regular basis?

Notes

PART 2 Resilience

In the second part of our four-part journey, we will use what we have gained from looking at self-awareness to dive deeper into becoming more aware of the barriers that prevent us from being more mindful communicators. The four chapters comprising this part of the book may very well present the darkest portion of our journey together, as we examine the prevalence of things like pride, ego, anger, holding grudges, forgiveness, and restoration of once-broken relationships. However, without understanding what ignites, inflames, and sustains conflict, we can't even begin to think about how to restore communication that has been broken. Instead, we must understand where the breakdowns occur before we know what approach to take toward fixing what has been broken. To do so is to build up our resilience toward such barriers that stand in the way of our most important relationships.

Our goals during this second part of the book are as follows:

- To assess the impact of pride and ego on our interactions with the self and others;
- To define and understand the characteristics that contribute to anger and ego buildup;
- To explain the causes for defensiveness and work toward reducing those causes; and
- To identify strategies for reducing anger, pride, and defensiveness.

CHAPTER 5

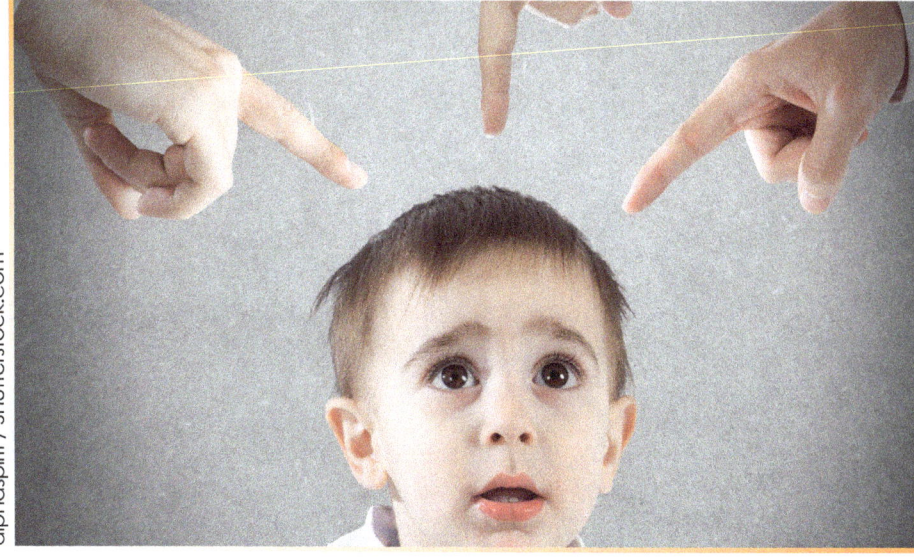

Judgment, Critique, and Ego

Fear is never a reason for quitting; it is only an excuse.

—Norman Vincent Peale

For most of us, the thought of defying expectations by doing something that pushes us out of our typical comfort zones usually results in feeling like the child pictured above, especially if what we want to do singles us out and invites stares, giggles, or worse, harsh judgment from those around us. Think about it: singing karaoke; dancing in public with a loved one, spouse, or partner; delivering a <gasp> speech; leaving the house without makeup or without doing one's hair; wearing comfortable yet unflattering clothes—all are often terribly anxiety-producing, depending on the person, of course.

The question we are then left with is, why? There's nothing inherently wrong with invoking your inner Freddie Mercury and belting out Bohemian Rhapsody with your friends in a crowded bar on a Saturday night. In fact, most of us would likely read that sentence and think, *actually, that sounds pretty fun*, but . . .

There it is: the BUT at the end.

As yourself: do any of the following phrases sound familiar?

- "Sure, I'd love to dance, *but* I'm not a very good dancer."
- "I love my pajamas/sweats, *but* I don't really feel comfortable going out like that."
- "Doing my hair takes so much time, and I need to get up so much earlier to do it, *but* I can't go out without it."
- "There's this girl/guy I'd love to ask out, *but* I'm afraid she/he would think I'm a total loser."
- "I love the beach, *but* I don't look very good in a swimsuit."

Think about what each of these phrases has in common. Better than merely thinking about them, let's systematically break these phrases down and look at the components each has in common:

1. **Agreement or acknowledgement.** an admission of positive (sometimes negative) value placed on the potential activity; "Sure, I'd love to dance/sing/be myself/date new people/hang out at the beach . . ."
2. **But.** a conjunction flagging the existence of a fear or anxiety preventing one from enjoying (or in negative cases, eliminating) the activity; ". . . but . . ."

3. **Assumption of judgment.** how we think others will hold us in negative esteem for having engaged in (or refrained from) such an activity; "... in reality, I'm afraid of what others will think when they see me dance/sing/be myself/ask someone out/hang out at the beach, and because I don't want to admit that openly, I'm going to invent an excuse that recuses me from any future invitations to partake in said activity."

> As-You-Are Activity: Before you read further, take a moment to think about times when you've gone through these motions. In the margins on this page (and more, if needed) honestly admit to examples of opportunities you declined simply because you wanted to avoid the potential judgment of others, and write them down. I'll start: Each of the above excuses was, indeed, one of mine.

Why in the world are we so afraid of what others think about us, to the point where we consciously limit life experiences for no other reason than to avoid potential judgment from others, even when that judgment may not even occur? Think back to Chapter 3 and the discussion on perception of self/others, as well as the Johari Window. So much of our self-perception is tied to what others think of us, whether we like or want to admit it or not. It's perfectly natural and normal for our self-perceptions to be affected by others, and admitting to the relationship between self and others' perceptions of us is not being weak. Rather, it is simply being honest.

However, knowing that others' perceptions of us contribute to our self-imposed limitations doesn't put an end to them. Instead, it only confirms what we already knew all along. How do we get to a point where the barrier of pride no longer gets in our way, but instead, we move forward and confidently do whatever we want? Part of the answer to this question is found through refining and revising the assumptions we hold regarding others' perceptions of us, and that is going to require a significant amount of courage from you and a smidgeon of trust in me, as I direct you to your next assigned activity.

Activity: One Less Bucket List Item

Think of one thing that you would love to do if you knew for a fact that nobody would judge you for doing it. Make it a good one, and more to the point, make it an activity you have never done. Perhaps this means that it's a bucket list item or maybe it's simply something fun that will present itself when the moment is right and you recognize those familiar feelings of anxiety because of others' potential judgment. Here are some ideas:

- Sing karaoke (bonus points for doing it completely sober);
- Dance in public without a care in the world;
- Do a poetry reading at a public open mic night;
- Go skydiving or bungee jumping;

- Go to a playground and play with reckless abandon like you did when you were a kid (bonus points if you do this one without taking kids along as an excuse);
- Do something crazy you normally would say no to: go to a nightclub with friends, play paintball, take part in a "polar plunge," take part in an intramural community sporting event such as dodgeball or softball, join a gym, take a painting class, so on; and
- Ask out that secret crush you've always dreamed of asking out, and do it confidently.

As you do this activity, focus on how it feels for you to break down pride and ego. More specifically, pay close attention to your evolving emotional state—very similar to the way in which you noticed your thoughts passing by like clouds in an otherwise blue sky—as you intentionally commit to the activity, leading up to doing the activity, while you do the activity, and how you feel following the completion of the activity.

Assumptions versus Reality

As of writing this book, I have been teaching public speaking for nearly a decade, and one thing never ceases to amaze and astound me. Students who confess to me their paralyzing fear of public speaking and their concerns that they will do horribly on their presentations rarely ever perform as horribly as their initial mental conception of the finished product. More to the point, they usually stand up in front of a group of 20 or so peers and confidently deliver well-constructed speeches, followed by telling me afterward how horrible they thought they did. Interestingly, with regular predictability, those very same students will also go on to tell me how amazing they thought their peers' presentations were by comparison! On the opposite end of that spectrum, I often fear for my more confident students who live under the impression that they can get by solely on their overconfidence, which usually comes across as cocky and arrogant, but more than that, unprepared, which usually turns off an audience faster than a light switch with a short circuit. What is it about the nervous students that cause them to do so well, while perceiving their performances as subpar? What is it about the overconfident students who do so poorly, imagining themselves as the world's gift to audience members everywhere, all while audiences perceive them as a presentation to be avoided?

    The answers to these questions exist within the queries themselves: it's all in perception. The nervous student perceives herself as somehow lacking and will do everything in her power to make up for that shortcoming by preparing and trying to eliminate all traces of uncertainty. Her perception generates a sincere concern for her audience, driving her to do whatever she must to fulfill the audience's needs. On the other hand, the overconfident student perceives himself as already complete and prepares nothing in hopes that his perceived completeness will overcome any content deficiencies. The nervous student is haunted by ghosts of her perceptions, most of which fail to come true because she has worked to prevent such a scenario from occurring. The overconfident student deludes himself by misperceiving the potential outcomes and swinging the pendulum to the other extreme.

    If, while reading this, you have already completed the *As-You-Are* and *One Less Bucket List Item* activities previously mentioned in this chapter, then you already have firsthand knowledge of how our perceptions and assumptions can create impassable barriers to otherwise exciting and desirable life experiences. This begins with the perceptions surrounding how we see ourselves:

- *I'm a horrible speaker.*
- *I have nothing valuable to say.*
- *I'm terrified.*
- *Nobody will be interested in anything I have to say.*
- *I'm the only person in the world who cares about this topic.*
- *They'll all think I'm dumb.*

The more we repeat this negative narrative, the truer it becomes in our own minds, as those perceptions become more firmly rooted assumptions regarding how others see us and, consequently, how others will react to us when we challenge those perceptions for ourselves. We become afraid that others will see us for the very fraud we imagine ourselves to be at the moment our self-perceptions are challenged.

Hopefully, as you completed the One Less Bucket List Item activity, you saw that nobody, or at least very few people, if any, even noticed you as you challenged the limits to your comfort zones. To illustrate this, allow me to share a couple of stories that serve as the impetus to this chapter's activities . . .

"Oops..."

Back in 2002, right after managing to convince one of the world's greatest women to say "I do" to marrying me, we moved out of town so that I could begin attending college as a nontraditional (AKA, old) undergraduate student. The town we moved to was Pullman, so that I could begin attending Washington State University. During the year in which we lived in Pullman before moving and switching schools (the reason for which is another story for another day, I'm afraid), I did not own a car. I didn't see a good reason to own one, since we lived only a couple miles away from the university, and I was healthy enough to walk back and forth to the campus each day. However, anyone who has ever been to Pullman knows that it's like a miniature version of San Francisco, but with winter conditions that rival that of Alaska, giving me the right to tell my kids today that, yes, I truly did walk two miles to school in the snow, uphill both ways.

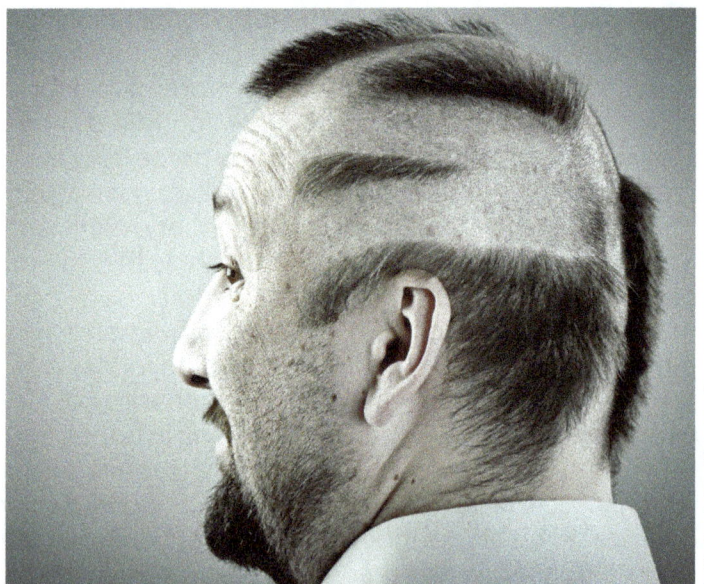

Note: Not a self-portrait

Anyway, during that time, I was rather particular about how I styled my hair. In fact, I was a downright perfectionist. I put so much product in my hair that it doubled as a helmet. The winter conditions, however, required me to wear a warm hat to keep my head warm and, in doing so, created a dilemma. Wearing the hat created the classic condition known as "hat-head," and I couldn't bear to remove the hat in class and suffer the judgment of my much younger peers for having bad hair, but on the other hand, I couldn't leave the hat on because my head would get so warm that, in between sweating profusely, I began to feel lightheaded.

My brilliant wife, who happens to be my beloved partner-in-crime, had a solution. She suggested purchasing a cheap set of home hair clippers from the big-box store and cutting my hair using one of the supplied guards so that I could take the hat on and off without worrying about the dreaded hat-head. While this seemed like a drastic styling change, and I was hesitant, I eventually agreed, and she clipped my hair clean off using the third-to-shortest guard in the box. Generally speaking, I was pleased with the outcome and felt good about the compromise.

This lasted about a month or so into the winter season, and she cut my hair about once a week to keep up on it. Looking back on it, I don't know why I couldn't cut my own hair, but again, that's another story for another day. Anyway, one evening, my wife was clipping my hair for me, with me seated on the floor in front of her on the couch, and I felt a tug on the top center of my head, accompanied by a loud buzz. "Oops," my wife said quietly. As she was clipping, the guard had fallen off of the clippers, effectively shaving my head completely bald in what can only be described as an inverse mohawk. I was mortified. I couldn't leave it like that, because that would require leaving my winter hat on all the time, even outside of school, to hide the mistake until it grew back in again, which would have been weeks at best. There was no other option. I had to okay her to buzz my entire head. Fear after fear went through my mind with each stroke of the clippers. People would judge me. Some might think I was a neo-Nazi skinhead. Others might assume I had cancer. Still more would assume I had lice. Regardless, it wouldn't be good, and everyone would stare.

But they didn't. Some of my coworkers looked at me with mild surprise and asked why I'd shaved my head, but that was the extent of others' reactions. My perceptions of the world came crashing down that fateful winter. Nobody had cared about my hair all along. My whole life was one big self-imposed set of lies at that point. I then began to wonder about all the other facets of my life or my personal appearance that I placed a high importance on, only to discover that I was the only one who cared or noticed in the end.

Pajama Outing

Not too long after moving away from Pullman and back to my wife's hometown in northern Idaho, yet another situation presented itself to me, allowing me to challenge my assumptions of how others perceived me. It was a classic sick day, wherein the whole family was feeling a bit under the weather, and my wife asked me to go to the store to pick up some needed supplies, like chicken noodle soup and soda crackers. Agreeing to her request, I got up and went into the bedroom. "What are you doing?" she asked, to which I answered by telling her that I was getting dressed to go to the store. "Why would you change?" she continued, "You're only going to the store. You don't really need to change out of your pajamas, just to come home and change back into them."

What she probably knew was that I still had a bit of my old self present, the one who wanted a carefully manicured presentation of my image while in public. Since we were back and living in her hometown, I would undoubtedly run into a member of her family, some of my peers, or worse, professors from my college! To see one of them while I was in my pajamas would be mortifying at best. I tried to argue with her that I had some other noble reason for changing, but as always, she was quick to see through my façade.

Note: Definitely not a self-portrait

She then dared me to go in my pajamas. Not being one to back down from a dare, I had to do it at that point. My pride was at stake, after all. So, I went in my plaid pajama pants and college hoodie, hiding my face from any potential people who I might know. As I walked through the parking lot and into the store, something struck me: nobody cared. Nobody stared at me, nobody pointed and laughed (not even small children), and not a single person made even the slightest snide remark like, "Nice pants, dude." I even ran into a fellow student and professor from my college! By the time I got home, suddenly much more comfortable in my pajamas, it seemed as though all my horrifying predictions were purely fictional.

I left the situation with the realizations that, yet again, my wife was right, but more than that I was gob smacked with the epiphany that all of my self-imposed constraints were strictly inventions of my own perceptions. There was not a solitary person anywhere in my world who either cared or even noticed when I challenged those perceptions and limitations. In the end, I came to understand that, though the race was long and arduous, it was only with myself; nobody else was participating in the competition for my self-esteem. These lasting lessons taught me that letting go of pride and allowing myself to freely challenge my ego was good not only for me personally, but also for my relationships. Learning to let go and take more risks was a process of regularly challenging my assumptions of how others thought and then reevaluating those assumptions after pushing my comfort zones further and further away. Taking those risks afforded me the opportunity to become a better all-around person for the sake of some of my most important relationships, a concept that we will explore further in coming chapters.

For now, however, ponder the following questions for reflection:

- Why do we allow our self-image to be so closely tied to what others think of us, especially when how we think others think of us turns out to be dead wrong?
- What does this potentially do for igniting, sustaining, and prolonging conflict? Do we act on assumptions, only to discover that doing so hurt the ones we love?
- Now that you've checked off a bucket list item and you felt how liberating it was to let go and do something you've always wanted, how might this open you up to taking more risks in the future, particularly with respect to relationships?
- Do you think you will be more likely to tell someone how you feel, ask for forgiveness, or restore a relationship that has been broken for far too long?

CHAPTER 6

The Poison of Pride and the Antidote of Forgiveness

I wondered if that was how forgiveness budded; not with the fanfare of epiphany, but with pain gathering its things, packing up, and slipping away unannounced in the middle of the night.

—Khaled Hosseini, The Kite Runner

In the last chapter, I asked you to do something brave, something crazy, and something that pushed the limits of what you thought comfortable or even possible. I asked you to consider checking off an item on your bucket list, throwing caution to the wind, and doing so without concern for the judgment of others. My intent in doing so was twofold. First, I wanted you to feel alive and throw off the shackles of those self-imposed limitations and judgments that we consciously believe others hold over us, simply to see that such limitations truly are created and maintained within our own minds. Simply knowing that such freedom is possible ignites a new confidence in us and emboldens us to try newer things and explore our new limits as though we were trying out a new pair of shoes for the first time. Second, however, I wanted to prep you for what was to come in this chapter. Brace yourself. It's almost time to tap into that newfound courage once again.

Before we get to that, however, let's begin with a brief definition of the concept of forgiveness, to make sure we're on the same page. Lewis B. Smedes, a renowned 20th century author and theologian, wrote extensively on the subject, and here are some of his more poignant quotes on forgiveness:

- "To forgive is to set a prisoner free and discover that the prisoner was you."
- "You will know that forgiveness has begun when you recall those who hurt you and feel the power to wish them well."
- "Forgiving does not erase the bitter past. A healed memory is not a deleted memory. Instead, forgiving what we cannot forget creates a new way to remember. We change the memory of our past into a hope for the future."

Other major thought leaders throughout history weighed in on the topic of forgiveness as well. Here are a few samples worthy of reflection:

- "Forgiveness is the fragrance the violet sheds on the heel that has crushed it."—Mark Twain.
- "Always forgive your enemies—nothing annoys them so much."—Oscar Wilde.
- "The weak can never forgive. Forgiveness is the attribute of the strong."—Mahatma Gandhi.

Forgiveness, in its purest form, is relatively simple; it is the act of accepting the fact that the past cannot be changed. When applied to interpersonal relationships, it becomes a mutual agreement to move forward together. In words, forgiveness seems simple enough, but in action, it becomes one of the most gut-wrenching and difficult tasks to endure.

Forgive, Forget, Sorry . . . What's the Difference?

What was the first thing to spring to mind when I mentioned the topic of forgiveness? Most people, when beginning a conversation on the act of forgiveness, will typically begin sharing painful personal stories with me about someone who wronged them in the past and how they've had a terribly difficult time moving forward and letting go of the harm that person caused. They will then typically begin talking about how they understand the need to forgive and possibly forget, but that they simply can't or haven't figured out how to just yet. For myself personally, the first time this question was ever posed to me by my Dissertation Committee Chair, Dr. Shann Ferch, that's the exact road my mind traversed before he asked me if I had ever thought about the difference between forgiveness-granting and forgiveness-seeking.

My first reaction to his query was something along the lines of, wait, what? Most of us, when faced with the cumbersome topic of forgiveness, immediately think of it in somewhat selfish terms. We want to know how *to forgive*, while forgetting that it's significantly more important, if not at the very least equally important, to learn *to be forgiven*. What causes our minds to almost automatically head this direction?

Part of the reason is due to us wanting to feel as though somehow our anger is righteous and justified. Whenever we are hurt, we want those who hurt us to feel similarly hurt, as though pain and suffering will somehow nullify itself if both parties are subjected to equal amounts of that pain. The idea of *granting* forgiveness is a concept we wrestle with because we end up concerned that, if we grant forgiveness to the person who hurt us, then it somehow gives permission for the other person to hurt us again in the future. In our minds, we picture forgiveness as handing over a get-out-of-jail-free card to be used in a future conflict, so in response, we resist, as if doing so will further punish the other person and cause him or her at least a fraction of the suffering we feel.

Seeking forgiveness is a thorny situation. To seek forgiveness requires us to engage in three critically important and yet, painfully difficult steps:

1. Step up as the first person in a conflict to begin reconciliation;
2. Outwardly acknowledge our role in the conflict; and
3. Make ourselves vulnerable by requesting forgiveness, knowing that a chance exists that such a request may be denied.

Most of us would rather endure a tax audit, a root canal, and a colonoscopy—simultaneously—than to have to do all three of these things.

Let's break down each step individually to determine why . . .

Step up as the first person in a conflict to begin reconciliation: Being the first person in a mutual conflict to speak up in the spirit of reconciliation is no small task. All too often, we get caught up in a conflict behavior we communication scholars like to call "kitchen sinking," which is exactly what it sounds like: dredging up old material from the past (likely material that had already been reconciled once before) and hurling it at our conflict opponent, even when—no, *especially* when—it has absolutely nothing to do with the current conflict. When a conflict has reached that stage, it generally becomes less about productively working through problems and more about who can hurt the other person with more violent efficiency. At some point, each person in the conflict has to retreat to a neutral corner to cool down, but who will be the first to come back and extend a peace offering?

More often than not, we resist being the first because we want to avoid being seen as weak. However, is that first person to offer a truce really all that weak, especially when doing so feels like we have to muster up all the strength we have left inside? If we pause for a second and think about what kind of impression another person might leave on us when that person consistently acts as the peacemaker, the first to apologize, and the one who actively ends conflicts—then that person is viewed as anything but weak. Such a person is often held in extremely high regard by all who are fortunate enough to have such a friend. Then, again, why do we view being the first to speak up as making us the weaker person? Such an attitude may arise from looking at a conflict as a battle or competition to be won. In such a perception, by being the first person to come forward, this results in losing or conceding; but, if we look at conflict using a different metaphor, such as a dance, where two people are moving together, then we see that the first person to come forward is the one who *leads*. It's all in our perceptions.

Outwardly acknowledge our role in the conflict: Once the olive branch has been offered and peace negotiations are underway, where do we begin? After all, if we continue to kitchen-sink the other person, then it will only serve to reignite the conflict all over again. On the other hand, we can't really begin by pointing out to the other person all the areas in which he or she was wrong during the conflict, because that also serves to stoke the still-smoldering coals. Simply put, we begin by acknowledging our role in the conflict by taking accountability and admitting fault. This is essentially the "I'm sorry" moment. This is the moment where I sincerely and honestly lay blame on myself for how I contributed to the creation, inflammation, and/or sustaining of the conflict by openly admitting and fessing up to each specific detail.

The key to success in this part is to avoid backhanded accountability statements, such as me saying, "I'm sorry I got so angry when you said I was being too sensitive, but you should know by now that I hate it when you say that." In this case, I could have simply said, "I'm sorry I got so angry when you said I was being too sensitive." The point is still made, but more importantly, the other person now has the opportunity to own up to his or her role in the conflict by potentially admitting that he or she knew that he or she should not have said that. Instead of pointing out where the other person went wrong, give that other person room to take accountability as well. Most of us don't like to have our faults proverbially pushed in our faces, and we will most likely react defensively when someone does just that. However, when given an opportunity to reciprocate taking accountability for our actions after seeing someone we care about take responsibility for theirs, most of us will take the honorable route and do so.

Side note: This is a great opportunity to point out that most of us stop at this point. We offer the olive branch, and then we say "I'm sorry for _____," but the reconciliation efforts typically cease after the apology. While the difference between saying we are sorry and asking for forgiveness may seem trivial, when experienced, the stark contrast between the resultant "feel"

of the two actions may as well be a chasm the size of the Grand Canyon. Saying sorry is usually received as little more than an admission of guilt. It involves owning up to our role in a conflict, but it cannot be the final word in restoring a relationship following a conflict.

Make ourselves vulnerable by requesting forgiveness: Taking an extra step to ask forgiveness presents a unique opportunity in that, in the moment of reconciliation, as we ask the other person to accept that we cannot go back in time and change our faults. Instead, we humble ourselves and momentarily place the other person in a position of power over us. The level of uncertainty that comes with this humbling step is fraught with anxiety, for in that moment, we make ourselves vulnerable. If the other person refuses, then our momentary humility will have been for naught, and the sting of rejection transforms our pain into shame. If the vulnerability gamble pays off, however, then our humility turns to elation, restoring the balance of power between the two individuals and returning the pair to a harmonious state. The resulting emotional overflow in such a moment can be powerful enough to reduce the hardest hearts to mush and the driest of eyes to a fountain of tears.

However, what happens if the other person refuses to grant forgiveness, for any reason? As mentioned before, if it is an outright and immediate refusal, then the sting of rejection can turn quickly to shame; however, we must remember that, even though we may be ready to seek forgiveness, the recipient of that request is in no way obligated to grant it. If the other person flat-out refuses, we must not insist upon immediate forgiveness, but instead, accept the decision and let the other person know that if and when the time comes when she or he is ready, then our request for forgiveness will remain open and without an expiration date. When we make our request to be forgiven, we must be prepared to allow time and space for the other person to contemplate and process the scope of what is at stake, as well as the implications of fully granting forgiveness. Rushed or forced forgiveness lacks authenticity and may prove hollow with time, so it is better to allow such a decision to be made carefully and mindfully. Forgiveness with purpose and intention, however, is *felt* and results in lasting resolution to a conflict.

Reconciliation

Forgiveness is not to be conflated with reconciliation. Forgiveness, as defined previously, is accepting that the past cannot be changed, while moving ahead with one's life. It involves a conscious and intentional refusal to allow a painful moment from the past to stay in our minds one second longer, rent-free. Reconciliation, however, is the restoring and healing of a relationship, often resulting from acts of mutual forgiveness. It is not, however, an automatic by-product of successful forgiveness. For example, a rape victim might eventually come to terms with the brutality of her or his assault and forgive the rapist, refusing to allow such a heinous act to dominate her or his thinking any longer, but such forgiveness can be granted without ever interacting with the rapist or notifying the rapist of said forgiveness.

Forgiveness without possibility of reconciliation is equally powerful, not only for the person granting forgiveness, but also for the person being forgiven. In 2003, at the sentencing of "Green River Killer" Gary Ridgway, a serial killer convicted of 48 murders of young women (who later confessed to twice that number), family members had their opportunity to speak directly to Ridgway. One after another, family members stood up and expressed their rage and hatred for Ridgway's crimes, and Ridgway stared all of them square in the eye, completely stone-face, and emotionally cold. But then, a grey-haired man with a long Santa-like beard and wearing rainbow suspenders named Robert Rule stood up and said the following, calmly:

> *Mr. Ridgway, there are people here who hate you. I'm not one of them. I forgive you for what you've done. You've made it difficult to live up to what I believe, and it is what God says to do, and it is to forgive. And He doesn't say to forgive just certain people, He says to forgive all. So, you are forgiven, sir.*

Before Rule's statement was finished, Ridgway's cold, hardened façade cracked under the unbearable weight of forgiveness breaking into uncontrollable sobbing. Where hatred failed to move Ridgway emotionally, forgiveness penetrated his heart, even if but for a moment.

> So, if forgiveness is great and its results healing, then why don't we do it more often? More to the point, what prevents us from seeking forgiveness when we know we are in the wrong?

Simply put, unhealthy pride is the barrier most often responsible for postponement, procrastination, or downright refusal to seek forgiveness. Pride, like forgiveness, however, can be looked at a number of ways. Healthy pride, which will be discussed later in this book, is good for us and a natural part of life. We feel it as parents, when we see our children accomplish a feat, we feel it as athletes when we break a personal best, and we feel it as students when our grades turn out much better than expected. Healthy pride provides us with motivation, it gets our positive hormones flowing, such as dopamine and serotonin, and it rewards us for a job well done. The question that remains, then, is in how healthy pride becomes unhealthy, which transforms into one of the most stubbornly difficult barriers to effective communication. Let's take a look at eight ways in which unhealthy pride presents us with such a barrier . . .

volkovslava/Shutterstock.com

    1. Unhealthy pride is driven to prove something. Unhealthy pride is often the outward result of self-doubt. This lack of self-confidence, combined with a fear of appearing weak to others, usually results in someone with an unhealthy pride "overcompensating" for what the person perceives as his or her shortcomings. As a result, such people often come across as cocky, arrogant, or bullheadedly stubborn. Resisting the responsibility to seek forgiveness often results from a desire to prove how right someone is, even when that person is wrong.

    2. Unhealthy pride results from taking too much credit. In instances of healthy pride, an individual may see herself or himself having won a series of small victories leading up to a major accomplishment, for which that individual can feel a justified sense of pride. However, in unhealthy pride, we see people demonstrating an equal measure of pride for modest or everyday achievements, or in even worse cases, taking pride in achievements that may not even belong to that individual. Again, this relates to hidden feelings of insecurity, which can also lead to feeling attacked by others, even within instances of constructive criticism. If such a person genuinely believes that he or she "won" a conflict, regardless of what it took to reach that point, then seeking forgiveness for any hurt inflicted takes away from that perceived victory.

    3. Unhealthy pride is disingenuous and inauthentic. Whereas healthy pride comes across as sincere and often paradoxically humble, unhealthy pride hogs the spotlight, boasts, and exaggerates accomplishments. The sincerity of healthy pride comes across as restrained and realistic. With unhealthy pride, humbling oneself and making oneself vulnerable are next to impossible.

4. Unhealthy pride is expressed loudly and aggressively and attempts to demonstrate superiority. Healthy pride is expressed quietly, allowing for others to notice, while unhealthy pride shouts to all who can hear, "Look at me and what I have done!" Most of us love to work with people who exude a quieter confidence, but most of us would much rather avoid someone showy who needs to be the center of attention at all times. Again, unhealthy pride refuses to "lower" oneself as a means to seek forgiveness.

5. Unhealthy pride demands attention. Closely related to the last principle, those with an unhealthy dose of pride demand to be seen, whereas those with a healthy sense of pride command attention by drawing others in like a gravitational field. People who exhibit unhealthy pride genuinely see themselves as victims, even in situations where they were the ones inflicting pain on others. They will often find a way to turn conflict resolution around on themselves to remain in the spotlight.

6. Unhealthy pride pushes others away for the sake of sole possession of all credit. While people who express pride healthily often deflect compliments and praise to the support team that made accomplishments possible, people exhibiting unhealthy pride will use "I" language to bestow upon themselves solo honors, effectively pushing away all other people who may have contributed to their success. On a large enough scale, especially in a position of leadership, such a person could become an authoritarian. Such people often assume they know more than anyone else, and their morally nearsighted perspectives are marked by a smug, self-aggrandizing sanctimoniousness and the belief that only they have the superior qualities necessary to be in control of others' lives. To seek forgiveness is to find common ground, which would require one exhibiting unhealthy pride to share the stage with others.

7. Unhealthy pride is wielded as a weapon of superiority. In cases of healthy pride, it is often used to inspire others to achieve their best as well, but in cases of unhealthy pride, we see any signs of success lorded over others and used to suppress any potential competition. Such people tend to view others who get too close as trespassers on their territory. This superiority prevents forgiveness-seeking due to the inherent humility required to do so.

8. Unhealthy pride is egocentric. Someone with a healthy sense of pride feels that pride for others when others succeed. If a work partner receives a well-deserved promotion, someone with healthy pride is naturally happy for that coworker and actively celebrates the promotion with him or her. Someone with an unhealthy sense of pride is more likely to exhibit symptoms of jealousy and rage, almost as though they feel slighted or passed-up, thinking that the promotion should have gone to them instead. As stated earlier, someone with unhealthy pride sees himself or herself as the perpetual victim and, as such, sees no reason to seek forgiveness from others.

Everything I know About Forgiveness, I Learned from My Dog

Allow me to begin this story by emphatically declaring that I am much more of a cat person than a dog person. I've always identified with the following quote from Robert De Niro's character in *Meet the Parents*:

> *You see, Greg, when you yell at a dog, his tail will go between his legs and cover his genitals, his ears will go down. A dog is very easy to break, but cats make you work for their affection. They don't sell out the way dogs do.*

I genuinely admire the way I have to earn a cat's love and affection. In fact, I have a cat at this moment who did not warm up to me for at least a few years, but once I earned her trust slowly and methodically, I became her best friend (until I rub her belly, and then all bets are off).

In a way, I suppose I can extrapolate something of myself when looking at my preference for cats. I tend to be somewhat guarded and protective of my trust at first for most people. I wait and watch what they do, carefully selecting who I allow into my "circle of trust," as De Niro's character would say, based upon how much of my trust I feel they have earned.

As a cat person, I suppose I've always looked at dogs with a healthy dose of skepticism. I never gave much thought to what De Niro's character said about "breaking" them, but I can't help but feel like dogs are a bit on the, well, dumb side. It's always seemed to me like dogs blindly offer their loyalty to their masters. Once you bring a dog home with you and give him or her some food, it's all over. You can tease them, toss them imaginary treats and laugh as they lunge at nothing, leave them alone all day long (knowing that they are waiting patiently by the door for your return), occasionally forget to feed them on time, and commit a whole host of other indiscretions, but their loyalty remains unfazed. There they still sit patiently, awaiting your return home again, ready to greet you with a wagging tail, and in my unnaturally large yellow lab's case, a cheesy smile (yes, he really does smile).

My beloved partner has always been the dog person in our family, and she absolutely adores them, which means I have to put up with them. As a result of healthy compromise in our relationship, she has always kept at least one dog, so I've had about a decade and a half to get used to dogs in our home and really observe how they interact. What has always struck me about dogs is their generally easygoing nature. I envy that.

Cats hold grudges. Make a cat angry by simply not filling their food dish up high enough (it doesn't even have to be totally empty for a cat to get irritated—just *near* empty) or by petting a cat the wrong way, in the wrong place, or at the wrong time, and the cat will not only let you know, usually in the most painful way possible, but will then spend the next several days knocking prized personal possessions and knickknacks off ledges and countertops. In a sense, I recognize that I've always been a little like cats in that regard. They say that people and their pets often hold striking similarities, and now, I understand why. When I get upset about something someone said, perhaps a sharp comment or an off-color remark, I have a tendency to ruminate on it, to allow it to occupy space in my head for hours and, even sometimes, days. I spin it around, look at it from various angles, and often end up stewing on what happened before finally confronting the other person much later, usually much to their surprise.

Dogs, on the other hand, forgive almost instantly. When our golden retriever sneaks a snack that may have been left out by one of my kids (something that happens often), we discipline her, usually by shouting "No!" At that moment, we clearly see her canine expression of remorse, as she cowers away to her doggy bed, tail between her legs. After cleaning up the mess, and I sit down near her doggy bed, she gets up, tail wagging, and approaches me, as if to say she is sorry. In that moment, I am absolutely dumbfounded by what is happening before my very eyes.

First, the way in which she approaches me, in the unassuming and humble way only a dog can, assures me she's already let go of what happened. She doesn't dwell on the way I yelled at her. She isn't fixated on rationalizing how she deserved the snack, nor is she making excuses for how she thought the snack was up for grabs. She doesn't "kitchen-sink" me by pointing out how this is the fifth time this week that I got angry and yelled at her for something. In that moment, what she exhibits is exactly the process described in this chapter. She is the first to extend the olive branch. She admits to her fault, as best a dog can without the benefit of spoken language, and, in doing so, seeks my forgiveness.

Second, I am struck by how her action is completely and utterly disarming for me. Regardless of how irritated or angry I might get, regardless of how indignant I might feel because she took something she *should have known better* than to take, and regardless of any of my other emotional baggage I might be holding (i.e., had a bad day, a headache, or tired), her selfless and humble gesture immediately softens me, and I forgive her. In that moment, she lets go, as do I, and we leave the past behind us (hopefully with her learning to no longer sneak those snacks).

In this sense, I have come to realize that we all have a lot to learn from dogs. Despite all our intelligence, science, critical thought, and advanced technology, it seems that we humans could take a cue from our dogs and be slow to anger, quick to forgive, and even quicker to seek forgiveness from others whom we have wronged. How wonderful would it be to become like a dog in this manner? To not ruminate over trivial offenses, to not waste precious time with loved ones by maintaining a divided relationship over some misunderstanding, or to be so filled with hateful, unhealthy pride that we avoid doing the right thing simply because we don't want to look weak? When reflecting on all of this, I am slowly being won over by dogs.

My cat is still my baby, though.

Activity: Forgive Like Fido

Remember when, at the beginning of the chapter, I mentioned that you would need to tap into some of the bravery you discovered you had during the last activity? It's time.

First, think of an unresolved conflict for which you would like resolution. Using principles of accountability, identify the roots of that conflict, but only the portions of that conflict that *you* own. Use the space below to write down all the ways in which you contributed to starting the conflict, inflaming the conflict, and prolonging the conflict:

_____
_____
_____
_____
_____
_____
_____
_____
_____
_____
_____
_____
_____
_____
_____

Second, set up a time to meet that person, preferably face-to-face, and if at all possible, over a good meal. Good, intimate conversation starts with time set aside and reserved for one another, and doing so over a meal only serves to isolate the interaction further, focusing your attention on one another. During this interaction, begin by recalling the conflict in general, but there is no need for you to rehash the entire ordeal. Once you both remember the conflict, then seize the opportunity to fully own *your* faults without placing *any* blame on the other person. Once you have successfully admitted to and owned up to your role in the conflict, as you outlined above, then take the final step and ask for forgiveness for your role in that conflict.

If this seems difficult, it's because it is. Such is the nature of conflict resolution, along with experiencing humility and vulnerability, but this activity is absolutely critical to your growth and development as a mindful communicator. We will build upon these lessons and experiences later in the book as well. If you need practice, perhaps consider trying this activity on a smaller, more everyday scale:

- Seek forgiveness for eating the last of the waffles, leaving your sibling or partner with no midnight snack.
- Seek forgiveness for yelling at your roommate or spouse for leaving the seat up again or not doing the dishes when it was their turn.
- Seek forgiveness from your child for the way you spoke harshly to her when she interrupted your work for the umpteenth time just to share a funny knock-knock joke she found online.
- Seek forgiveness from your parents for forgetting to call as often as you perhaps should.

Regardless of how you approach this activity, do so with courage and equipped with the knowledge that you are learning to become a leader within your most important relationships, because, as the first person to step forward and take responsibility, you are setting an important precedent in your relationships. Don't be at all surprised if the other person almost immediately reciprocates your lead and asks for forgiveness from you for their role in the conflict as well. Just don't expect it going into the activity.

When you're done, reflect on the following questions for thought:

- Why do you think you hesitated to seek forgiveness in this situation?
- What usually prevents you from seeking forgiveness?
- How did it feel to release yourself from pride, anger, and guilt, as the act of forgiveness took place?
- How likely are you to incorporate asking forgiveness in your relationships in the future?

CHAPTER 7

Listening—The Greater Half of Communication

There are many benefits to this process of listening. The first is that good listeners are created as people feel listened to. Listening is a reciprocal process - we become more attentive to others if they have attended to us.

—Margaret J. Wheatley

Throughout our modern educational system, regardless of what state or country we have been educated within, one thing about communication education becomes painfully obvious. Our educational system, from elementary education to higher education, places emphasis on learning to communicate with others, through public speaking, working in small groups, or talking with others one-on-one. But, such education focuses mostly, if not completely, on messages leaving the individual and heading toward a receiver—outward communication. Few aspects of education, if any, focus on learning the other half of communication—**the more important half**—that of learning to listen. The Greek philosopher Epictetus, in 55 A.D., said, "We have two ears and one mouth so that we can listen twice as much as we speak." That being stated, it would seem that we should probably spend more time on studying the art of listening.

Before moving on, however, an important though obvious distinction to make is that listening is not the same as hearing. When we hear messages, sound waves modulate our eardrums in and out, producing electrical impulses that are sent to the brain and registered as sound. Hearing is a remarkable passive activity that anyone with working ears can conduct without effort. Listening, on the other hand, is remarkably active in nature. It involves processing sound into bits of information and then stringing those bits together to form messages. Adding this to our nonverbal observation abilities, we weave together the message with peripheral (though simultaneous) communication cues, such as tone, facial expressions, gestures, posture, and other nonverbal cues to construct not only the literal meaning of a message, but all the collateral meaning associated with the way the message was presented. In other words, it is not only what we say, but it is how we say it. To become great listeners requires training, practice, and commitment, but more than that, it requires us to accept above all other truths that listening requires effort. Of course, some styles of listening require more effort than others, and that is why we must learn to recognize the different styles of listening, as well as which styles are better to use in various situations.

Every single one of us exhibits each of the diverse listening styles at various times; though generally speaking, we tend to gravitate toward one specific style best suited to our personalities and communication styles, and then we stick to using that style most of the time. Dr. Roberta Turnbull-Ray (1994) proposed eight categories of listening styles, each of which requires varying amounts of effort, as well as concern for other people vs. concern for oneself. The following self-quiz, developed by Turnbull-Ray, will help you identify which of the styles tends to be strongest for you, and we will discuss what that means for us later in the chapter. For now, grab something to write with, and take the following self-quiz. To gain an accurate assessment, however, you need to be as honest as possible, even if doing so could paint you in a bad light!

Listening Inventory

For the following 40-question survey, read each statement carefully, and then reflect for a moment before deciding whether that statement describes the way you usually feel, sometimes feel, or rarely feel.

Part 1

1. I can listen well and have little difficulty understanding and remembering when a supervisor is explaining a new procedure that I will be using my job or when a sales person is explaining how to use some equipment that I am purchasing, such as a computer or television.
   Usually ☐   Sometimes ☒   Rarely ☐

2. I find many speakers and subjects boring and irrelevant to my concerns.
   Usually ☐   Sometimes ☒   Rarely ☐

3. I am only interested in subjects that directly relate to my job, my business, my finances, my hobbies, or my family.
   Usually ☒   Sometimes ☐   Rarely ☐

4. After listening to someone make a long statement in a meeting or give a speech, I tend to remember specific details, statistics, or examples, rather than the central idea and main arguments.
   Usually ☐   Sometimes ☐   Rarely ☒

5. It would be generally easier for me to list some facts the speaker gave than to state her/his central idea.
   Usually ☐   Sometimes ☒   Rarely ☐

Part 2

1. Whenever I am trying to persuade people, I make a point of trying to discover what they believe and why before I give my arguments.
   Usually ☐   Sometimes ☐   Rarely ☒

2. I am able to listen courteously and carefully to people with opposing viewpoints to understand why they feel the way they do, and I can ask follow-up questions to encourage them to elaborate on their reasons for believing or acting as they do.
   Usually ☐   Sometimes ☐   Rarely ☒

3. I am able to listen to people express views, opinions, or ideas to which I am strongly opposed without feeling threatened, angry, or defensive, and without feeling that I must interrupt and give my opinions before they finish speaking.
   Usually ☐   Sometimes ☐   Rarely ☒

4. When trying to sell products, I listen primarily to determine what my customers need and why they might hesitant to buy a product.
   Usually ☐   Sometimes ☒   Rarely ☐

5. I like to encourage people to talk about their hobbies or whatever interests them.
   Usually ☐   Sometimes ☒   Rarely ☐

Part 3

1. When I answer the phone at work, I prefer that the caller comes to the point immediately.
   Usually ☒ Sometimes ☐ Rarely ☐
2. If someone asks me about a sermon or lecture I heard the day before, I am able to state the speaker's purpose and summarize the main ideas.
   Usually ☐ Sometimes ☐ Rarely ☒
3. I enjoy listening to a wide range of topics as long as the speaker is well organized and knowledgeable, and I find relatively few topics too boring or difficult.
   Usually ☐ Sometimes ☒ Rarely ☐
4. As I listen to a speaker, I tend to summarize mentally what the person has been saying and to anticipate the next major point she/he will make.
   Usually ☐ Sometimes ☒ Rarely ☐
5. I listen for central themes rather than isolated facts, and I like speakers who challenge me mentally.
   Usually ☐ Sometimes ☒ Rarely ☐

Part 4

1. Even though I have strong convictions about a particular topic, I am willing to listen to arguments on the other side.
   Usually ☐ Sometimes ☒ Rarely ☐
2. I have to admit that I frequently hear sound, intelligent arguments in support of positions I don't agree with.
   Usually ☐ Sometimes ☒ Rarely ☐
3. I find it frustrating when speakers omit crucial issue while discussing a topic.
   Usually ☐ Sometimes ☒ Rarely ☐
4. Whenever we listen to someone, there is a *thought/speech-time differential* because listeners can think at a rate of 3–4 times faster than speakers can talk. While listening to a speaker, I use this differential to determine whether the speaker's arguments and main points clearly support her/his thesis and whether there are any inconsistencies in the message.
   Usually ☐ Sometimes ☐ Rarely ☒
5. When listening to persuasive messages, I try to determine what are the values, principles, or beliefs upon which the arguments are based.
   Usually ☐ Sometimes ☒ Rarely ☐

Part 5

1. I find it difficult to listen to criticism without becoming angry or building a defense automatically.
   Usually ☐ Sometimes ☐ Rarely ☒
2. I find it difficult to admit that I am wrong when I am actually wrong.
   Usually ☒ Sometimes ☐ Rarely ☐
3. I find it difficult to handle certain loaded words that invoke strong emotions.
   Usually ☐ Sometimes ☒ Rarely ☐
4. If two people are whispering something in a corner, I assume they are saying something bad about me.
   Usually ☒ Sometimes ☐ Rarely ☐
5. I am quick to notice personal attacks on me or subtle criticisms of my work or behavior.
   Usually ☒ Sometimes ☐ Rarely ☐

Part 6

1. I fake attention and only pretend to be listening to coworkers, friends, or family members, while I am actually daydreaming or thinking about something else.
   Usually ☐   Sometimes ☒   Rarely ☐
2. I find it difficult to stay alert and concentrate on what is being said when listening to a speech or lecture that lasts more than 30 minutes.
   Usually ☒   Sometimes ☐   Rarely ☐
3. I believe that the speaker has primary responsibility for holding my attention, and I should not have to work at resisting distraction.
   Usually ☐   Sometimes ☒   Rarely ☐
4. I listen best to speakers who are humorous and entertaining.
   Usually ☒   Sometimes ☐   Rarely ☐
5. In conversations with family or friends, I find myself cutting off the other speaker before her/his point is made, or responding by changing the subject.
   Usually ☒   Sometimes ☐   Rarely ☐

Part 7

1. People interest me, and I tend to pay close attention to the people I meet in both social and work situations.
   Usually ☐   Sometimes ☒   Rarely ☐
2. When listening to people I have just met, I try to determine what interests and motivates them.
   Usually ☐   Sometimes ☐   Rarely ☒
3. Although I may form quick judgments about people based on their behavior when I first meet them, I realize that first impressions are often wrong, so I consciously look for behaviors that may indicate that my initial assessment needs modification.
   Usually ☐   Sometimes ☐   Rarely ☒
4. I pay attention to nonverbal communication, noticing the silent messages people send with their posture, gestures, and facial expression, and I notice when people are sending double messages (i.e., their tone contradicts their words).
   Usually ☒   Sometimes ☐   Rarely ☐
5. I am interested in observing how people act under pressure and how changing circumstances may influence their behavior.
   Usually ☐   Sometimes ☒   Rarely ☐

Part 8

1. I feel comfortable when people show their emotions or express their feelings in my presence.
   Usually ☐   Sometimes ☐   Rarely ☒
2. When someone tells me about a problem she/he is having, I am able to listen patiently without making judgments, giving advice, or interrupting.
   Usually ☐   Sometimes ☐   Rarely ☒
3. I am able to express my feelings and emotions in the presence of someone I trust.
   Usually ☐   Sometimes ☒   Rarely ☐
4. When listening to someone expressed strong feelings of joy, anger, fear, or grief, I feel as though I am sharing the emotion with her/him.
   Usually ☐   Sometimes ☒   Rarely ☐
5. I would describe myself as warm, spontaneous, and responsive to other people's feelings.
   Usually ☐   Sometimes ☒   Rarely ☐

Scoring the Listening Inventory

Go back to Part 1, and give yourself 5 points for each "Usually" response, 3 points for each "Sometimes" response, and 1 point for each "Rarely" response. Add up the total score for Part 1 and write it down below. Repeat for Parts 2–8. Most people take this assessment score highest in one or two parts. Take note of which parts scored the highest and which scored the lowest.

Part 1: 15
Part 2: 9
Part 3: 15
Part 4: 13
Part 5: 19
Part 6: 21
Part 7: 13
Part 8: 11

↑ High Task	**Part 1:** Detailed Listening	**Part 2:** Persuasive Listening	**Part 3:** Comprehensive Listening	**Part 4:** Analytical/ Critical Listening
	← Narrow Scope of Listening		Broad Scope of Listening →	
Low Task ↓	**Part 5:** Defensive Listening	**Part 6:** Superficial Listening	**Part 7:** Personality- Oriented Listening	**Part 8:** Empathic Listening
	← Concerned with Self		Concern for Others →	
	← Passive listening, low effort		Active Listening, high effort →	

FIGURE 7.1 Listening Inventory
From The Power of Listening by Roberta Turnbull-Ray, Ph.D. Copyright © 1994 by Kendall Hunt Publishing Company. Reprinted by permission

Detailed Listening

As we take a look at Figure 7.1, we see that *detailed listening* is positioned in the high task, narrow scope, concerned-with-self segment of the matrix. Detailed listeners are on a mission. They are listening for specific points, such as instructions. A fast-food restaurant worker who was just hired uses detailed listening to learn the rules of the organization and how to work the equipment. Detailed listeners tend to be proficient at remembering complicated sets of instructions, grocery lists, birthdays of friends and family members, and how to complete other complex, ordered tasks. However, detailed listeners often miss the bigger picture and have a harder time conceptualizing big or abstract ideas. For example, a college student who tunes out everything a professor says because she is listening only for material that will be on the exam will have a hard time understanding how each detail relates to one another. Such a listener has all the pieces to the puzzle, but no idea how they all fit together.

Persuasive Listening

Moving from left to right on the top row, *persuasive listening* employs high task, a slightly broader scope, and a slightly increased concern for others, but still primarily focused on the self. The level of effort increases in this type of listening, as their primary mission is to listen to information that will help their persuasive task, such as closing a sale or earning a vote. In a sense, their main directive in listening is still self-focused, but persuasive listeners tend to pick up more from others than mere task details. Persuasive listeners make great salespeople, politicians, and skilled negotiators.

Comprehensive Listening

Comprehensive listening remains high task as with the prior two styles, but it crosses the centerline of the table into a greater concern for others than with oneself. Additionally, the level of effort increases significantly over persuasive listening, and the overall scope broadens more completely to encompass a greater portion of the speaker's message. Comprehensive listeners tend to focus on learning and understanding the main ideas behind a speaker's perspective, and their level of interest includes a wide range of speakers and topics. Comprehensive listeners are great at piecing together conversational puzzles to determine the ideas motivating a speaker's message, but often at the expense of the details due to the broad scope of their style. That stated comprehensive listeners often make the best students, for they are able to piece together the components of a lecture to not only recall those pieces, but also to understand how they fit together. For example, a nursing student who is a detailed listener may do great on an anatomy and physiology exam when forced to regurgitate the names of various body parts, but a nursing student who excels at comprehensive listening will be able to understand how each part works in tandem with others, allowing her/him to more effectively perform the nature of the job later in life.

Analytical/Critical Listening

Being in the upper-right quadrant of Figure 7.1, *analytical/critical listening* requires the highest degree of mental effort and concern or focus on others, the broadest scope, and remains task-focused. This type of listening, most often used by those skilled in debate and argumentation, requires one to master the skills requisite of persuasive listening as well as comprehensive listening, because, to analyze and be able to critique a speaker's message, the analytical/critical listener must be able to not only pick apart the message, but also to understand the whole of the idea or message being presented. Analytical/critical listeners are often distracted by errors of reasoning, but tend to respect well-informed arguments and sound use of reasoning. Since this style of listening requires a high degree of mental effort, it can also be highly exhausting. Those with experience in debate can speak to the level of fatigue one experiences after a particularly challenging debate. These types of listeners often take advantage of the thought/speech-time differential. Most of us speak at a rate of 125–150 words per minute, but we are capable of thinking at a rate of over 500 words per minute, giving us plenty of time to reflect on and consider the message someone is saying to us. Careers suited to this type include attorneys, politicians, investigators, professional negotiators, and mediators.

Defensive Listening

On the opposite end of Figure 7.1, we find *defensive listening*, which is the most harmful style of listening to interpersonal relationships. Being in the lower-right quadrant, this style is not concerned with task, requires little-to-no effort, is passive by nature, has a narrow scope, and is fully enveloped in oneself. Defensive listeners perceive threats all around them and are primarily concerned with protecting their egos at any and all costs. These types of listeners often have "triggers" that, when heard, regardless of speaker intent or context, send them off into what we might call "attack mode." What started out as something innocent can quickly end up blown out of pro-

portion. Employing this type of listening causes us to act erratically and irrationally, and we may even devolve into what is termed "kitchen sinking," which is the act of dredging up old (often previously resolved) conflicts and using them against someone, even if completely irrelevant. Once defensive listening has been engaged, it is often best to disengage from the interaction, as listening has effectively ceased and anything one says can and will be used against them.

When defensive listening sets in, it prevents us from concentrating rationally, partly because our minds shift to a highly emotional and volatile state, nearly devoid of reason and rationality. Additionally, when we become defensive, we increase the odds of the speaker mirroring our behavior and becoming defensive as well. Some people carry unresolved and ignored emotional pain around with them like baggage, and in an effort to project that pain onto others, they listen defensively, looking for opportunities to lash out and make others hurt as well. In stark contrast to other listening styles, defensive listening has no redeeming qualities and is purely harmful.

Superficial Listening

If you have ever allowed your mind to wander during class, staring out the window while daydreaming about a Bermuda vacation during a dreary midwinter lecture, you have engaged in *superficial listening*. While not exactly as harmful to relationships as defensive listening, superficial listening can still cause damage to interpersonal relationships, particularly if doing so becomes a noticeable habit. Superficial listening requires almost no effort (if anything, the lack of effort is the hallmark of superficial listening) and seems to have a focus almost completely on oneself. Even though this style appears further to the right of the spectrum in Figure 7.1, don't let its positioning deceive you; for superficial listeners, it's all about themselves and doing as little work as possible. Most of us tend to slip into superficial listening when feeling drained or fatigued. Boredom can also trigger this style. Additionally, we can become distracted by a speaker's looks, clothing, mannerisms, or voice. Something as small as a stain on a speaker's shirt can be the trigger for superficial listening to take place. Unlike other styles, this type of listening bears no positive rewards, although it is not as potentially hazardous to one's relational health as defensive listening.

Personality-Oriented Listening

Crossing over the centerline of Figure 7.1 again, *personality-oriented listening* requires a greatly enhanced concern for or focus on others. This style involves listening with the intent to understand what drives or motivates others and how one can be more responsive and relatable with them. This style of listening can be thought of as the persuasive listening style, but instead of a focus on a self-motivated drive to persuade others (high task, focus on self), this style is centered on others and learning how one can be more effective in relation with them. This type of listener makes a great friend or loved one. This listening style is of great importance to newlywed couples or even couples who have mutually expressed a desire to be monogamous and committed to one another in the long term, because this style helps them learn more about one another and how their personalities mesh with one another.

Empathic Listening

Last on the list of listening styles is that of the style with the highest degree of effort required, combined with the highest concern for or focus on others: *empathic listening*, which may also be called therapeutic listening. The purpose of this intense and sometimes difficult style of listening is to help others and empower them. Similar to the analytical/critical listening style, empathic listening is absolutely draining and exhausting, so it should be used sparingly, only when the moment calls for doing so. It involves listening deeply and sincerely feeling what others feel, while mirroring emotional states of the speaker and using those states not only to understand the speaker on a deeper level, but also to help the speaker understand her/his own emotions.

Four steps help develop empathic listening:

- Attending behaviors: These are our nonverbal cues that signal we are actively paying attention–eye contact, head nods, direct body orientation, leaning toward the speaker, etc. These behaviors tell a speaker that we are interested and encourage the speaker to continue.
- Reflection: Similar to a reflection in a mirror, the empathic listener is able to paraphrase and restate a speaker's message without adding judgment or inference, but it is done so through the use of attentive silence, waiting for the most opportune moment to reflect back to the speaker, so as not to interrupt.
- Clarification: Listening carefully to the message, the empathic listener is able to determine which parts of the message need further information, articulation, or elaboration, and asks follow-up questions to keep the speaker sharing the message in greater detail. Clarification is clearly sought as a means to greater understand and empathize with the speaker.
- Perception-checking: This is a technique that involves the empathic listener checking with the speaker to ensure the way the message has been heard is the correct interpretation—"If I understand you correctly, you are saying that you feel like I haven't been listening fully to you lately?" Perception-checking is done out of goodwill and not in an attempt to entrap the speaker; in other words, it does not incite defensiveness, but rather, comes from a place of understanding and humility.

As important as it is for empathic listeners to dive into a conversation with the full intent of feeling what the speaker is feeling, it is equally critical for empathic listeners to understand the importance of taking care of oneself in between listening sessions, for empathic listening can take a toll on one's emotional well-being. Empathic listeners fit best in organizations when employed as counselors and therapists, although many go on to work in social work and volunteering to help marginalized communities as well. Any career that takes advantage of their strong innate desire to listen to and help others will benefit from the employment of empathic listeners.

Recognizing the Need for Each Style

As mentioned previously, each of us engages in every one of these listening styles at one point or another, but we all tend to naturally gravitate toward one or two of the styles most of the time. However, by learning to recognize the benefits of each style (save for the defensive and superficial styles, of course), we can learn to control our styles, effectively employing a style more suited to the context requiring our attention. For example, when sitting in on a college lecture, we can recognize the need for comprehensive listening to better retain not only the important details, but in how they all weave together to form a bigger picture. When being trained on a new task at work, we can employ detailed listening to better recall individual details in the job at hand. If a friend comes to us with a life-altering problem, we can employ empathic listening to alleviate our friend's suffering. Being able to recognize the needs required in the moment is at the very core of what it means to be mindful and immersed in the present, and furthermore, adjusting our listening style to suit those needs allows us to apply mindfulness to the greatest good.

Activity: Hanging on Every Word

Choose a person with whom you would like to improve communication, and seek out an opportunity to have an uninterrupted conversation without the need to rush. Try not to overplan it, but rather, simply watch for an opportunity to present itself. As you have this conversation, use your imagination to put yourself in a place where you pretend as though this conversation was the last conversation you might ever have with this person. Of course, don't be melodramatic about it—this isn't method acting.

Octa corp / Shutterstock.com

Instead, use your imagination to put yourself in a mental state wherein you hang on every word as though it was among the most valuable pieces of information you have ever heard. Treat this person's thoughts as though they were fragile, delicate trinkets, handling them with great care. Ask clarifying questions to keep the person talking, and do your best to continue demonstrating a sincere interest. Pay special attention to how the interaction differs from others you may have had with this person in the past.

CHAPTER 8

Vulnerability and Accountability

Vulnerability is not weakness. That myth is profoundly dangerous.

—Brené Brown

Rosalind Russell once said that acting feels like "standing up naked and turning around very slowly." Think about that for a second. Roll it around in your mind in the same way you might swish around a fine wine or savor exotic cuisine.

Go ahead . . . we have time.

Now, let's talk about the way that quote makes you *feel* when you first read it. If it felt creepy, awkward, slightly uncomfortable, or perhaps rekindled previously suppressed memories of a 7th-grade nightmare where you showed up to school in your underwear, then what you just experienced was *vulnerability*. Vulnerability is essentially risk of getting hurt in some way. Vulnerability might also refer to our openness or willingness to risk emotional pain, as in being both willing to love and be loved in return, all while accepting the emotional risks that go with being in love.

Vulnerability is what we feel . . .

- In the quiet moments before speaking to someone we find attractive;
- Asking someone we like out for the first time;
- Right before the first time we tell someone those three little words;
- Moments before delivering a speech to an unknown audience;
- When asking a boss for a raise (or, in some cases, simply asking for a day off);
- On the first warm day of summer, as we disrobe at the beach;
- The first moment when, as a new first-time parent, we stare longingly, lovingly into the eyes of our firstborn child, realizing that nothing will ever be the same again;
- Realizing that we did something wrong and hurt someone we genuinely care about;
- Recognizing that, as a result of hurting someone we care about, we need to make it right.

Vulnerability is best described by once again looking at dogs. When a dog has respect for her person, she will roll over and expose her belly, which in her perception, is potentially dangerous if she didn't already trust that person. Okay, so maybe she does this more as a hint for a belly rub, but still, her instincts compel her to automatically do this as a way of saying, "I'm not threatening because I'm exposing my most vulnerable parts to you and lowering all my defenses." Dogs do this to demonstrate trust and respect, but are we humans all that different? We'll get to more of that later in this chapter, but for now, let us look at why the vulnerability weakness persists.

Most people, especially men, think of vulnerability as the polar opposite of confidence and strength. To be vulnerable is to appear weak, fragile, overly sensitive, or even fearful. As mentioned before, dogs make themselves vulnerable to submit—becoming submissive in the process—and as humans, we tend to associate submissiveness with a negative, dark quality, because submissive people are less confident, scared, timid, squirrely, sheepish, and . . . vulnerable.

In her book, *Daring Greatly*, Brené Brown wrote, "vulnerability is also the cradle of the emotions and experiences that we crave." Naturally, we are drawn toward experiences that provide us with love, belonging, creativity, courage, joy, hope, empathy, connection, and authenticity, and it doesn't take a tremendous amount of thought to connect the dots between vulnerability and these emotions that make life worth living. Brown went on to define vulnerability as "uncertainty, risk, and emotional exposure." When we start to think about vulnerability in these terms, we recognize that, to be in a worthwhile relationship with someone who requires us to put ourselves out there for our partners to see, opening ourselves up to uncertainty (Will they love us the same way we love them?), risk (What if they don't reciprocate the way we feel about them?), and emotional exposure (What does it say about us if they don't require?). Ultimately, vulnerability is terrifying because it is the culmination of all the what-ifs we can possibly think of, and sometimes, that realization is scary enough to paralyze us from ever acting in a vulnerable state. We become so scared of the potential for a negative outcome that, in a sense, we create a negative outcome by prolonging the inevitable, a self-fulfilling prophecy, if you will.

Accountability

Vulnerability has a sibling that goes by the name of *accountability*. Admittedly, there are times in our lives where we are unequivocally at fault. Few of us are able to recognize when we are the ones to blame, and even fewer people among those are able to take the next step and admit being the root of a problem.

Personally, when I was younger (in my teens through to my mid-20s), I thought that being wrong or making mistakes was the worst condition in which I could possibly ever find myself. In my mind, if the people around me whom I cared for deeply never saw me make a mistake or trip up somehow, that I would earn their undying respect. In reality, later in life, I discovered that it was quite the opposite. I would often go to such great lengths to prevent having to accept blame and admit fault that I was pushing away those whom I cared for deeply, and to be perfectly honest, I can't say that I blame them. Few of us like to be around perfect people, and even fewer of us want to be around someone who thinks he's perfect, because in our estimation, that is the epitome of arrogance—and that's how others used to see me.

Chad Zuber / Shutterstock.com

It wasn't until I started paying more attention to the people in my life who I admired most that I realized there was a benefit to this thing called accountability. As I began observing people I respected more carefully, I started noticing that they were quick to accept blame, even for the smallest, most trivial mistakes, and in doing so, they demonstrated not weakness or self-doubt, but a high degree of self-awareness and humility. Sometimes, it even seemed like they would take the blame as a way of allowing others to save face, even when they weren't the ones at fault, and this baffled me.

Nevertheless, I started experimenting with accountability on my own. I started small, admitting to forgetting various tasks throughout the day, apologizing for miniscule mistakes at work, or even by approaching my professors and admitting to the very same mistakes they pointed out in my papers. What resulted from these interactions surprised me. My professors, most of the time, would take a second look and retract their comments or offer to allow me to resubmit revised versions for additional credit. Other times, they would take the time to offer more advice on how to strengthen my writing or how to think more deeply or critically for the next paper. My boss at work started opening up and becoming more personable with me. My wife even began joking about how forgetful I tend to be, rather than getting so upset about my tendency to be absentminded. In other words, as I grew in accountability, I experienced the opposite of what I feared would happen, and in that, I discovered the paradox that accountability breeds trust and openness in relationships.

The relationship between vulnerability and accountability can, at times, be complex, but for the most part, is easy to understand. To demonstrate, let's take a look at a real-life example from my own experience . . .

While I don't recall the specifics leading up to the incident, the outcome remains clear in my memory. My youngest son, who was nine at the time, was persistently interrupting some work I was trying to get done on the computer in his quest to grab my attention, and in my frustration, I snapped at him, doing so angrily enough to elicit a few stray tears. As he walked away, gazing at his feet and still crying quietly, I immediately recognized the crossroads at which I had arrived.

One turn at this intersection involved me being self-righteous and justifying my behavior by growing indignant and telling myself that I am our family's sole income, that my students depend on me to get my work done in a timely manner, and that my work deserves my full, uninterrupted attention to give it my best. Above all else, this turn hinged on the fact that I am his father, and therefore deserved to have my will respected and obeyed.

The other turn, however, involved me attending to my self-awareness and recognizing that my child takes priority over my work. When I work from home, I have the luxury of allowing such interruptions on occasion, and I recognize that, when my child interrupts me, he is doing so because whatever he has to share with me is important enough in his eyes that he wants to invite me into sharing it with him. I also recognize that my snapping at him only serves to lessen any future desire he may have to share similar treasures with me down the line, and that I only snapped because I was being selfish with my time.

In the end, I (wisely) chose the latter of the turns at these proverbial crossroads, and I sought out my son immediately, seeking forgiveness from him. In doing so, I had to make myself vulnerable and admit fault, setting aside any fear I may harbor of him thinking less of me because I admitted making a mistake in judgment. By admitting fault, I demonstrated to him that it is perfectly okay to make mistakes, as long as we are willing to own those mistakes later and seek forgiveness from anyone who was harmed by that lapse in reason.

One of the most profound lessons in accountability came to me by way of a story I was told by my doctoral dissertation chair, Dr. Shann Ferch, who frequently recounts the following story about the man who would later become his father-in-law:

> *He had made a sharp comment at the dinner table to his wife. I didn't even pick up on it. In my family, on a 100-point scale of verbal violence, his comment was a -8. After dinner, he came over to me and said, "I'd like to ask your forgiveness for the way I treated my wife at the dinner table."*
>
> *I didn't know what to do. I said, "Ah, you don't have to ask me."*

And he said, "No, I don't ask just for you. In our family, we ask forgiveness of the person whom we harmed, and also everybody who was there, in order to restore the dignity of the one who was harmed."

That moment, combined with his investment into my life, changed me entirely.

Accountability not only serves to restore the honor of the person seeking redemption, but also the dignity of all those affected by the lapse in judgment. Nowhere in my life was this more evident that a day that would serve to forever change the way I looked at vulnerability and accountability. It all started with a cold day in Chicago, where I, along with my teenage daughter and youngest son, marveled at the snowfall on the tarmac. Looking out the window, I joked to my daughter, "Who's going to shovel all that snow off the wings before we take off?" A little part of me inside grew worried by the minute, because I knew that the harder the snow fell, the better the chances were for a delay.

Sure enough, our delay came. I refused to let it bother me, as I was intentionally trying to demonstrate patience to both my daughter and six-year-old son accompanying me on our trip back home. This was a remarkably hard task, considering that, in the last three days, I had acquired a cumulative four hours of sleep. Regardless, I kept cool with an ounce of pure determination, mixed with a dash of stubbornness.

I ended up sleeping through most of the preflight delay, as did my children, but it wasn't until about 30 minutes before landing that panic set in. The flight attendant announced that, because of the delay, we would arrive at 11:00. Looking at the boarding pass for my connecting flight, I realized it was scheduled to take off at 11:02.

Two minutes.

Knowing there was no way I would de-plane in time with two children in tow (from the back row of the plane), I gave up and prepared for the worst. However, the flight attendant, overhearing me discuss with the kids that we would miss our connection, announced to the rest of the passengers to let us go first and as such, remain seated until we got by them. She then used her personal Wi-Fi connection to locate our gate, which was in a completely different terminal.

Two minutes.

It was going to be close, but for some strange reason, I thought that if this young woman refused to give up, then I shouldn't give up either. Summoning my last remaining fragment of tattered determination, I decided we would give it a go.

We landed, and the sound of seat belts unlatching and carry-on bags zipping broke the silence. The flight attendant announced one more time for everyone to remain seated and let us off before they turned off the seat belt light. The ding from the light going off might as well have been a starting pistol, though. As soon as we stood up to begin our mad rush, so did everyone else. The other passengers ignored the attendant's instructions and went about their day, meandering slowly and taking their time to gather bags, to put on coats, and to perform other menial tasks.

We were the last ones off the plane.

I began to feel enraged at seeing this outpouring of selfishness and willful ignorance. My determination to make the connection was growing by the millisecond, though, and as soon as we were out of the gate, the three of us sprinted—or at least, as fast as six-year-old legs can run.

Reaching the terminal and seeing our gate within grasp, I felt a glimmer of hope, but that hope dissipated when I realized the jet bridge door was closed, the reader board had been updated to reflect the next flight assigned to the gate (which wasn't ours), and the seats surrounding the gate were empty.

Two minutes. We missed our flight because of the two minutes we lost due to the brash selfishness of others. My outrage turned into an outright grown-man-tantrum.

I spotted a ticket agent at the desk in front of our gate, and struggling through gasps to catch my breath, I shouted in his direction, "Excuse me!"

He turned to see me, only to turn around again. The bastard ignored me. "Hey!" I shouted again, breathless and exhausted, "Can you help us?"

"Sorry, but I can't help you right now," he responded, turning his back and walking away from the gate.

This was the last straw. My temper boiled over like scalded milk in a pot too small to contain it, and I lost it, shouting angrily, "Well, that's just [bleeping] great! How the [bleep] are we supposed to get home now?"

The agent sped up, but turned his head slightly back toward us and in a hurried matter-of-fact manner, replied, "If you missed your flight, go see the automated service counter between gates C2 and C3!"

Automated service counter? First, we miss our flight because of selfish airline passengers, now I'm being ignored by the only customer service employee I can find, and he wants me to use an impersonal computerized system to figure out my predicament for myself? "Stupid piece of [bleep]," I muttered to myself, in reference to the fleeing agent.

That's when I looked down and to the right. There was my six-year-old, looking up at me. He wasn't looking for answers to our problem. He wasn't looking at me because I was being loud, self-righteous, and indignant. He was looking at me because he had never encountered a situation like this before in his young life, and he needed to find a way to deal with it, should it ever happen again.

The problem was, I was giving him a precedent. My childish tirade presented him with a solution to his future conflicts when dealing with difficult situations and even more difficult people.

Long story short, I found the self-service station, and it took me all of 60 seconds to scan our tickets and print out boarding passes to another flight, four hours later than our original departure. We now had the time to eat lunch, relax for a while, and most importantly to ponder how I was going to reconcile what I had just instilled in my children.

I needed redemption, and it had to be something they would remember.

For the next three hours, I simmered and stewed, allowing my anger to lift like a fog that the sun cuts on a cold, clear winter morning. Contemplate as I might, the best course of action I could come up with was a brief lecture on how it isn't right to lose your temper with others when it isn't even their fault, but I knew that a lecture would be likely to go in one ear and out the other. I needed something that would stick.

Roughly 30 minutes before boarding our new flight, that's when it came to me. I chose to do something daring, something that I normally wouldn't have done, and it is something that I will never regret, as long as I live.

As soon as I had spotted the original ticket agent, who was working the desk at our gate again, I leaned over and told my daughter what I was doing and asked her to watch our bags for a few minutes. As she agreed, I grabbed my son's hand and said, "Come with me."

"Why, Daddy?" he asked as he looked up from playing a game on my phone.

"Just come with me," I replied, "I need you to watch and listen."

He got up, held my hand, and walked with me across the carpet to the desk. There was a line of passengers, and we waited. My heart began thumping against my ribs, and my palms formed a thin film of sweat. When it was our turn, the agent looked up at me and asked, "Can I help you?"

I doubt that he recognized me, or at least, it didn't seem like he did. I approached the desk with my son's hand in mine and said:

"Sir, I don't know if you recognize me, but about three hours ago, I did something inappropriate. I cursed at you because you didn't help us find a new flight after we missed our connection, and that wasn't right. I took my frustration out on you and set a poor example for my children. I want to apologize to you and ask your forgiveness."

He looked stunned. He was speechless and still for what felt like forever, and just as I was ready to turn and walk away, he spoke:

"I don't know what to say. I didn't hear you use any foul language, but I do remember you. At the time, I was trying to locate a medical kit for a woman boarding her plane over at the gate next door, and I was in a rush. I wanted to stop to help you, but I was in a hurry to assist the passenger over there. I'm sorry I didn't stop to help."

I became even more ashamed of my actions. I responded, "You have nothing to apologize for, sir. I was in the wrong, and I need to ask forgiveness to right this wrong, but also to show my son that the way I behaved was not right."

Again, in disbelief, he looked stunned. "It's okay. I forgive you, and I cannot tell you how much I appreciate your apology. You didn't need to do this. Quite frankly, nobody ever has, and trust me, we get yelled at a lot in this job. You just made my day, and I thank you for that." He then extended his hand to shake mine and said, "My name is Ron."

Grabbing his hand, I replied, "Thanks, Ron. I'm Josh. Nice to meet you, and I hope you have a wonderful rest of your day."

Turning to walk away after giving Ron a smile, I looked down at my son, who was still gripping my hand tightly. He was staring up at me again, but this time, doe-eyed, with the beginnings of a smile. I smiled back at him, tears brimming on my eyelids, and said, "That, my son, is doing the right thing. Always do the right thing, no matter what."

Five minutes later, Ron called me back to the desk over the loudspeaker. After I sat back down, he had looked at the flight manifest and noticed that the three of us were in separate rows, spread out all over the plane. He took the initiative to not only rearrange people to allow us to sit together as a family, but also moved us to seats with additional leg room.

Forgiveness is a gift of love, an act of beauty that benefits not only the person being asked by way of reconciliation, but also the person requesting it, by way of redemption. Thanks to snow, a delayed flight, and the self-interest of others, I had the chance to make things right and to set in motion a lifetime of redemption for my children. To do so required me to be vulnerable, to face all the fears and what-ifs, and then stare them down and take a gigantic risk, which, in the end, paid off more than I ever could have expected.

Where to Begin

Now, it's your turn for an exercise in accountability. Using the communication audit activity from Chapter 4 as our starting point, choose just one of the areas for improvement that you identified as a result of your time alone. As you reflect on this one issue or area for self-improvement, articulate self-responsibility in the problem and reflect on how taking accountability can help solve it. Summarize below how pride and ego have contributed to the conflict, but also consider how they might have prevented you from resolving the issue up to this point. Assign yourself a firm deadline for approaching the problem (not necessarily solving it) with courage and conviction, and then stick to that deadline. Above all else, focus on taking responsibility for your role in whatever the issue may be and approach this with honest, raw vulnerability.

For example, if I identified social media addiction as an issue that I'd like to address, I might take accountability for how often I allow myself to succumb to a desire to check social media, which usually gets in the way of my flesh-and-blood interactions, seeing as how my nose is buried in a screen, and I'm unavailable for others around me. Furthermore, I might try to identify recent conflicts, where someone tried to point it out to me (like my wife, who is really, really good at that), and I became defensive and denied having a problem. To address pride and ego, I might start keeping an objective record of how often I am on social media by logging every time I check it, so that I might challenge my own defensiveness with self-awareness. Furthermore, I might examine how my behaviors impact those around me by talking to them and asking for their insights into how they perceive my behaviors. Lastly, I might assign myself limitations, such as taking one day or more off of social media per week, or limiting my social media time to a specific time period each day, thereby freeing up my attention for the rest of the day.

Notes

_____
_____
_____
_____
_____
_____
_____
_____
_____
_____
_____
_____
_____

PART 3 Savoring

In part three of our four-part journey, we turn away from the darkness that comes with examining resilience to the various barriers that prevent us from not only becoming more mindful, aware, and present, but also those that prevent even our most basic conditions of happiness and fulfillment. Instead, we now turn our attention toward an exploration of the qualities that make life worth living, the study of which falls within the domain of *positive psychology*. Now that we are well versed in intrapersonal communication, listening styles, and how to prevent anger, pride, and the ego from taking over, we need to look at more active and preventative strategies for restoring communication, which is where positive psychology comes into play.

Our goals during this third part of the book are as follows:

- Examine the experience of savoring the moment and discern the four types of savoring;
- Explore the impact of sharing positive interpersonal growth with others;
- Actively assess your orientation toward gratitude;
- Describe the impact of gratitude on perception; and
- Articulate the connection between mindfulness, savoring the moment, appreciation, and interpersonal relationships.

CHAPTER 9

Savoring the Moment

During the last night, I savor once more the intimate relationship we have established with our planet. Shivering in the pilot's seat, I have the feeling I have left the capsule to fly under the stars that have swallowed our balloon. I feel so privileged that I want to enjoy every second of this air world. During our three weeks of flight, protected by our high-tech cocoon, we have flown over millions of people suffering on this earth . . . Why are we so lucky? . . . Very shortly after daybreak, [our balloon] will land in the Egyptian sand, Brian and I will be lifted away from the desert by helicopter, and we will immediately need to find words to satisfy the public's curiosity. But, right now, muffled in my down jacket, I let the cold bite of the night remind me that I have not yet landed, that I am still living one of the most beautiful moments of my life. The only way I can make this instant last will be to share it with others.

—Dr. Bertrand Piccard
A Swiss physician who traveled nonstop around the globe in a balloon, along with British copilot Brian Jones.

Mention the word *savor*, and most of us likely conjure up images of slowly stuffing our faces with rich chocolate cake, sinking our teeth into a juicy rib eye, sipping a glass of fine wine, or maybe even biting into an apple, peach, dark-red cherry, or juicy ripe pear plucked straight off the tree. I admit, I salivated a bit as I typed those out just now. Perhaps, however, savoring doesn't have to invoke memories of great food or drink; maybe we think of a hot bubble bath after a hard day at work, relaxing with a good book before bed. Speaking of bedtime, perhaps we imagine ourselves sinking into a pillow-top mattress borrowed for the night within an upscale hotel room. Regardless of what we think, the end result is the same: Savoring is a heavenly activity, generally invoked by some pleasurable sensation not to be missed because we were too distracted to notice it. Savoring involves slowing down and paying more mindful attention to the sensations we experience, and in most cases means that we try to make the feeling last as long as possible.

However, what I just described above is only one aspect of the concept of savoring. Before I move ahead to describe the other types of savoring, as witnessed in the example quote from the beginning of this chapter, allow me to share the story of how I came across this fascinating concept of savoring, a construct that, once learned, changed the course of my research and writing focus indefinitely.

Discovery

The year was 2008, and I had just been accepted into the Doctoral Program in Leadership Studies at Gonzaga University. Upon my acceptance, I was advised to begin considering what I would eventually settle on for a research topic, because the program, like so many others, required that each student performs a unique research study that contributes something novel to the field of leadership research. For me, the general area of emphasis was fairly obvious; I wanted to study mindfulness. As a result of one of my other stories (see my story about revealing my blind spot at the beginning of Chapter 3), I recognized that the concept of mindfulness had done more to change my life—as a husband, as a father, and as a general human being—than anything I had ever learned up to that point. The topic of mindfulness alone, however, was simply too big. I had to narrow and focus it to be more manageable, and more importantly, I had to make a connection to leadership somehow.

A wise adviser of mine suggested that I keep a journal of my ideas. Whenever I had an idea for a research study, regardless of merit or value, I should write it down in the journal. Over time, he said, the journal would reveal certain patterns of thinking to me, and the topic would simply reveal itself. So, I opened a text file on my computer and began brainstorming ideas: mindfulness & teaching, mindfulness & public speaking, mindfulness & creativity, etc. The list went on for what seemed like an eternity, and yet, still, I had no firm direction. I had been warned that whatever topic I decided upon should be something I was head over heels in love with, because in a sense, I would end up being married to that topic for up to seven long years. As you can imagine, a doctoral student picks the wrong topic, and divorce from that topic (and the person's sanity) would be imminent.

It happened one evening in a flash of brilliance, an epiphany if you will. I was getting on the freeway, heading to campus, when I suddenly realized that I should combine two areas I was in love with: mindfulness and fatherhood. There was only one problem: My drive to campus was about 30 minutes long, and I was too excited to get there so I could start researching whether other scholars out there had done such studies before (it's okay to call me a nerd at this point—I've accepted my lot in life). So, while on the freeway, I started refining my topic by thinking about instances of mindfulness that impacted my experience of fatherhood, and I immediately thought about situations where it seemed like the rest of the world simply faded into obscurity and only my children and I remained. Such moments are not only memorable and rich with emotional experience, but also become a reminder of what makes life worth living. In those moments, I felt an overwhelming sense of gratitude for what was happening, so I determined that I wanted to study how mindfulness could facilitate gratitude among fathers and their children, and what impact such gratitude might have on their relationships. The connection to leadership seemed like a no-brainer, given that most of us acquire our first conceptualization of leadership from watching our parents. I eventually arrived on Gonzaga's campus and began searching around, and to my surprise, *nobody* had ever conducted a study even remotely like the one I envisioned, and that's when I officially married my research topic.

I got so excited about it that I bought my newfound topic its first honeymoon present. I applied for and won a grant that afforded me the opportunity to buy no less than 25 books on the topic of gratitude from Amazon, and believe it or not, I read every last one of them (eventually). The problem, I discovered, was in the definition of gratitude. Every last author of every single book said essentially the same thing. Gratitude is the result of a giver providing a gift to a recipient. However, my kids weren't giving me anything in the moments I wanted to study! They were simply there, I was there as well, and we shared the power and beauty of these moments together without any sort of gift exchange. For months, I wrestled with this seemingly major speed bump that had slowly morphed into a full-fledged brick wall.

The saving grace came in the form of a textbook publisher representative who, on any other day, likely would have been regarded as the annoying yet-necessary scourge of academia, or the well-dressed used-car-sales-type professionals who come to a professor's office occasionally to attempt to persuade him to adopt their overpriced textbook for their classes. The irony of you reading that sentence within such a textbook at this moment is not lost on me, by the way. Anyway, the rep in question showed up at my office just as I was leaving to go to class at Gonzaga, and as usual, he asked whether I needed anything. Half-jokingly, I told him my contextual dilemma, and he laughed at the coincidental nature of the fact that he just so

happened to have a positive psychology textbook in his bag as a sample. He recalled seeing that it had a section in it on gratitude and offered it to me as relief for my situation. I took it, put it in my bag, and headed for my evening class. Having arrived a bit early, I retrieved the book from my bag and immediately went to "gratitude" in the index. I turned to the page referenced, partially with hope and somewhat cynical, only to find the exact same definition I had discovered in 25 other books on the same topic.

However, the very next heading under this section on gratitude was a Times New Roman, 12-point font, bold term: **Savoring**. The very sight of this word stopped me cold. I put the book down, shook my head a bit, and thought, *this is it . . . this is what I've been searching for*. As I picked up the book and read further, that's when I discovered not only the definition of savoring the moment that so perfectly and in sublime simplicity described what I had been experiencing with my children all along, but then it broke down the general term into four subtypes of savoring, all of which served to clear the painfully obtuse fog that had been holding up my progress for months. What I had experienced was not necessarily gratitude. It was savoring.

General Savoring

The academic definition of savoring is: to attend to, appreciate, and enhance the positive experiences in one's life. While this definition gives us a good starting point, we need to expand it further. The essence of savoring is to fully immerse oneself in appreciation for the experience of the moment, thereby shifting one's attention from objective reality to the subjective interpretation of the experience. Still, that can be a lot to take in, so let's think about it like this: Savoring is the act of fully appreciating an experience as it unfolds by noticing the way that experience affects us in the present. Savoring is capable of stretching our perception of time to create a relative experience of time (i.e., generally describing time as having come to a standstill, "time flies when you're having fun," etc.), but also may be experienced in anticipation of an experience leading up to a pleasant experience, during the experience itself, or in reminiscing on an experience from the past. Now that we have established a basic understanding of savoring in general, let us turn our attention to the individual characteristics that go into a moment marked by savoring. The act may be described in four distinct processes that regulate positive emotional states: basking, luxuriating, thanksgiving, and marveling.

Basking

It was a chilly day in October, and my youngest daughter was playing at her third volleyball game of her seventh-grade year. She and I worked tirelessly in our backyard on her overhand serve, which was something she wanted to achieve and perfect, as few of her peers were able. She wanted to stand out and accomplish something hardly any of her peers had by that point, and I was happy to oblige in helping her achieve that goal. My daughter stepped up to the line to deliver her first serve, and sadly, it fell short, narrowly missing the back of one of her  teammates' head. She looked up at me in the bleachers with disappointment, but shrugged it off as if to say, *next time*. Eventually, the game wore on, and her turn arrived again, but still, her serve came up just barely short, getting nicked by the net. By the third serve, she had reached an optimal state, because she knew just how much harder she would have the hit the ball to put it where she wanted it to go. Tossing the ball up into the air, her right hand coiled back around like a cobra ready to strike, and at the perfect time, bam! She smacked the ball, sending it clear of the net and dropping in the middle of the other team's players, who were all stunned and unprepared. Not only did my daughter make it over the net, but she did so and scored an ace, which was something none of her teammates had accomplished, at least not with an overhand serve. As my daughter found me in the stands and locked eyes with me, her excitement and joy became infectious, and I could not help but beam with pride for what my daughter had accomplished.

What I experienced in that moment was the aspect of savoring known as *basking*, or savoring as a result of pride. Basking is an internal response to an external stimulus, such as the result of either receiving praise oneself or seeing a loved one receiving similar accolades. We quickly internalize basking as the sensation of pride, and the sensation can easily be prolonged, especially when referencing the self with others (as in winning a championship game and seeing the losing side suffer the agony of defeat), referencing the self with the past (as in achieving a new personal best or attaining a long-awaited goal), continuous flattery from others, or when basking is applied to people with an already-elevated self-esteem. Basking tends to come at a cost, though, as basking too much can easily be interpreted as arrogance, or it can flat-out become egotistical behavior if engaged too frequently. Frequently, many of us might resist basking simply because we worry that doing so could be construed by others as excessive pride, so it is often stifle as a result. Finally, basking is one of the savoring behaviors that is not subject to habituation, meaning that one could hypothetically bask in the same level achievement repeatedly without losing much of the effect.

Luxuriating

The type of savoring initially referenced at the beginning of the chapter (i.e. food, drink, a hot bath, etc.), and the type we most often think of when referencing the word, *savoring*, is that of luxuriating. To luxuriate is to simply savor the experience of a pleasurable physical sensation (taste, touch, smell, sight, sound, or some combination thereof). The smell of fresh-brewed coffee in the morning, the crisp, cool air of a fall morning, getting caught up and swept away while listening to one of our favorite songs, and even sexual release are all forms of luxuriating.

Luxuriating is strongest when experienced in comparison with an opposite state, such as the sudden release of stress or as a reward for hard work. Again, like basking, this is an internal response to an external stimulus, but unlike basking, luxuriating is significantly harder to prolong and is far more prone to habituation than any of the other forms of savoring. Too many bites of ribeye or glasses of the same fine wine will drastically reduce the sensation of savoring. To enhance this form of savoring requires that we convince ourselves that we are deserving of such luxury and pampering, such as feeling like we deserve a reward for something. However, as with basking, overdoing luxuriating comes at a significant cost by making the person more hedonistic and sending that person in search of greater pleasures to achieve the same effects.

Thanksgiving

This form of savoring is essentially what its very label connotes. Thanksgiving is when we acknowledge or express gratitude for blessings, gifts, or favors of some kind. We perceive a giver offering something of value to us (the giver need not be human—it is possible to be grateful for nature, for good weather, to a pet for companionship, etc.), and in return, we offer a humble, reverent reflection and usually an outward expression of our appreciation. Unlike basking and luxuriating, we can experience thanksgiving not only in reaction to an event, but also

proactively in anticipation of a gift or favor. Thanksgiving can easily be prolonged, depending on the contextual circumstances, and we can enhance it by comparing our situation to alternative outcomes in which we might not be as fortunate. Thanksgiving is also considerably less likely to end up with habituation, since gratitude is less likely to be something we grow

Marveling

I intentionally saved this form of savoring for last because it's not only my favorite form, but also the one that played a starring role in inspiring most of my research. To marvel is to be rendered speechless with awe, and it is one of the single greatest experiences of the human condition. To become awestruck with marveling is to lose all sense of self and time, for the world to melt away, and to be left with whatever external stimulus jolted us out of an otherwise tedious or mundane existence. Such moments include the following:

- A majestic sunset that seemingly ignites the sky;
- Holding one's newborn baby for the first time and gazing into his/her eyes;
- Standing in front of a magnificent work of art and being enraptured by the raw talent captured by the artist in each stroke;
- A heart-stopping vista atop a mountain that you see just as you turn the corner, noticing all of nature spread out before you;
- Spending still, quiet moments with a loved one where it seems as though the rest of the world has disappeared, leaving you alone with this person and an awe-inspiring wellspring of emotion.

Such were the moments of fatherhood that I wanted to study. I found that, the more mindful I became as a father, the more of these moments miraculously seemed to appear.

However, marveling, unlike the other three forms of savoring, is remarkably fleeting and difficult for us to intentionally create through choice. While a regular sense of mindful presence and curiosity lay the groundwork for such situations to arise, marvel has to occur naturally and spontaneously. One cannot simply decide to be marveled, although two conditions can be present and plant the seeds for marveling to grow organically. Those conditions are vastness and the need for accommodation. *Vastness* refers to something in which we, as observers, recognize as being significantly larger than ourselves or at the very least, larger than what we might consider ordinary in our experience. *Accommodation* refers to experiences for which we cannot make sense, and we end up being forced to accommodate a new understanding. Accommodation is not always achieved, but instances of awe produce a need for us to at least try to accommodate. If the experience escapes understanding, it can leave us terrified (think Paranormal Activity), while understanding reached as a result of accommodation generally produces positive sensations of enlightenment. Marveling can produce a diverse and volatile mixture of emotions, creating feelings of chaotic dissonance through the combination of fear, amazement, dread, confusion, but at the same time, it instills feelings of empowerment and optimism.

As such, marveling tends to be the most intense form of savoring, yet also the shortest-lived and most prone to habituation. Intuitively, this makes sense. One can only experience holding one's newborn child for the first time once. That remarkable sunset that caught your eye is never coming back the same way again. The second time you visit the Grand Canyon is not as great as the first. This leads us to the only drawback to this type of savoring, which is experienced through feelings of loss, sadness or regret for losing the moment as it passes, or feelings of insignificance in comparison to the event itself.

Wonder, or the result of the experience of marveling, may be likened to emotion as adrenaline is to physiology: a short-lived burst of intense emotional power that can dramatically shift one's short-term perspective. Awestruck moments that facilitate marveling and a sense of wonder are more likely to affect our perception of time during this type of savoring, as well as have a potential destressing effect, particularly if we are currently experiencing high stress, such as a looming deadline. One well-documented example of the effect of marveling on perception of time occurred while in Earth's orbit, as NASA mission specialist Laurel Clark described a fleeting moment of experiencing a sunset in space: "There's a flash; the whole payload bay turns this rosy pink. It only lasts about 15 seconds and then it's gone. It's very ethereal and extremely beautiful." This 15-second period of time produced what she described as one of the most memorable moments of her career, and as an astronaut, that's saying something.

While habituation does occur for marveling if the exact same moment occurs repeatedly, these moments are considerably more unique and prone to chance, making them difficult to control and reproduce. As such, moments of marvel are fleeting, paradoxically pointing to a more limited chance of developing habituation. Regardless, by cultivating a regular sense of mindful presence and curiosity, marveling can be evoked at some of life's simplest experiences; not all have to be grandiose. As a father, some of the most memorable moments I have are of times when I was simply struck by noticing the curiosity of youth unfold through discovery, such as watching my daughter chase a ladybug around the backyard one day, squealing with glee all the while.

The Impact of Savoring on Interaction

Now that we have a better idea of what savoring is all about, how it happens, what enhances it, and what potential danger there is in taking it too far, what do we do with this knowledge? It's intuitively easy to understand that savored experiences in the presence of others lead to greater interaction. For example, a random night of my misspent teenaged youth sticks out in my memory to this day, and for seemingly no discernible reason. Three friends and I spent a warm summer evening sitting around a beat-up picnic table talking about life, telling jokes, and generally just living in the moment without a care in the world. Nothing remarkable took place, no major event marked the occasion, and I certainly don't recall the date (I'm even having trouble remembering the year, to be honest). In talking with others and retelling this story, I have become vindicated by hearing similar stories from almost everyone who has ever heard me tell them about the night in question. So, let's analyze what's going on here.

First of all, let us break down the conditions that fostered the growth of such savoring. First, such situations usually involve one of more good, close friends, or at least people with whom we feel a strong connection or relation. Second, dialogue is also a part of the formula, but it's not any old run-of-the-mill everyday conversation. This dialogue is usually described as being in a state of what Mihaly Csikszentmihalyi (Me-high Cheek-sent-me-high) dubbed "flow"—a state free of restrictions and more analogous to dancing, where disruptions in the flow of interaction are kept to nil or at least a minimum, and participants in the dialogue seamlessly play off of one another's statements. Topics of these conversations may wander frequently, but do so smoothly and nearly without participants noticing. Third, distractions are nearly eliminated, leading to a state of mutually mindful presence. This partly accounts for the distortion of the perception of time, as all conscious focus is trained on the interplay of the moment, rather than on future or past events. Fourth, this awareness leads to an appreciation of the value experienced within the moment. Rather than looking back later on the moment and reminiscing (though that does occur), participants recognize the worth experienced and traded throughout the interaction, and that recognition and subsequent gratitude deepens and enriches the quality of the interaction, regardless of content. It has been said that such interaction has a tangible glow to it, and once participants "see" that glow and latch onto it, savoring of the moment has begun.

Activity: A Savory Meal

Now that we know the components that cultivate savoring (good people, dialogue in flow, no distractions, and appreciation), let's conduct an experiment to see whether savoring in any of its four forms (or a combination thereof) is something we can potentially create.

To conclude this chapter, I want you to have a <u>good</u> meal with someone you genuinely care about. This means no fast food, no TV dinners, no ramen, and no stovetop mac-and-cheese. It should be either a meal that requires careful time, planning, and preparation (think soul food here), or a quiet, elegant restaurant meal that doesn't involve the wait staff coming out and randomly singing birthday songs to its patrons. Regardless of how you choose to set up this meal, ideally, it should involve truly memorable food and conditions that reduce distraction.

During this meal, focus on savoring the moment, practically as if the world will end once it is over. How would you treat this moment if you knew it would never happen again? Be natural though, and don't be overly dramatic about it. Bask in your conversations, laugh with reckless abandon, and savor each bite of your food slowly. The most important thing here is to savor each and every second you spend with that person.

Don't be surprised if it doesn't blow your mind, though. Many people naturally savor time spent with loved ones on a regular basis, so if you're one of those, then this will be just another meal with friends or family for you. Others may get hung up on the thought of this being their last chance to spend time with that person. Still more may try too hard at making the conditions just right, only to find that the moment was "meh" and fizzled out before savoring had a chance to begin. If this happens, relax. Perhaps you give it another go at a better time or with better company. The important thing is to keep trying until you feel like savoring has taken place.

Questions for Reflection

Once savoring over a good meal takes place, then try to identify and describe what, if anything, made this interaction stand out from others like it in the past. What does the simple act of mindfully creating opportune conditions do for savoring the moment, and what does this do for your ability to communicate on a totally different level? What would happen if you applied this more often? What is currently stopping you from doing so?

Then (and this is the hard part), using what you know now about mindful presence and savoring the moment, think about a situation from your past, where you wish you had applied these techniques, and in doing so, try to reflect on how the outcome may have been different, if you had only slowed down to savor that moment.

CHAPTER 10

Must Be Present to Win

Prediction belongs to the future. Analysis is the property of the past.

Action is the sole prerogative of right now.

—Dr. Josh Misner

In the last chapter, we first explored many nuances of the concept of savoring, including what triggers the various forms of savoring and what enhances them as well. We also discussed the conditions necessary for savoring to take place, the primary and fundamental building block of which is that of mindful presence. It almost seems to go without saying that, if we are not intentionally tending to the present moment, we will miss out on opportunities to savor, seeing as how we will not likely recognize them, due to our focus being placed elsewhere. Like the great Ferris Bueller once said, "Life moves pretty fast. If you don't stop to look around once in a while, you might miss it." Therefore, it seems only apropos that this subsequent chapter takes a look specifically at the intersection where mindfulness meets savoring. Since it is a building block, without which savoring could not happen, it seems an accurate place to aim our curiosity to the moment where mindfulness blossoms into savoring, to better understand how to cultivate such moments that make life worth living.

As such, instead of having our chapter activity occur at the end of the chapter, I want you to take part in the activity first this time, before you continue. Ready for it? Here we go . . .

Activity: A Lens to a New World

For this activity, you will need only two materials: a camera and some free time (preferably alone). A smartphone with a decent camera will work perfectly fine, but you may use either a digital camera or an old-school film camera as well. As for the free time, plan for at least an hour, but be advised that in this activity, it is incredibly easy for time to run away from you quickly. I've done this activity before where it ended up running about three hours, and it wasn't until my wife texted me a "Where are you?" message that I realized how long I had been gone.

Here are the step-by-step instructions:

1. Ideally, familiarize yourself with the camera before heading out. The more familiar and comfortable you are with the camera's settings, the more effective this exercise will be. You won't want to spend all your time fumbling with various settings, so be sure to brush up on them before going. If you don't have the time or the know-how, simply use whatever automatic setting seems best.

2. The day you head out should ideally be a relatively sunny day. If you live in the Pacific Northwest like me, you grow accustomed to a stark lack of sunshine, but having a wide range of light significantly enhances this activity. This isn't absolutely necessary, so don't stop reading for a week while waiting for better weather. It can certainly be done indoors if needed, but a sunny day provides more light from which to choose.

3. Go to a relatively quiet and calm location away from where you live, such as a park or out in the country. You're aiming for a change in scenery that also aids in reducing distraction. Once you get to where you want to be, find a comfortable place to wait for an extended period of time, whether sitting or standing, and then simply stay put and visually scan the area for a while, patiently and intentionally. Take time to pause and notice everything in your immediate surrounding. Notice the curves and recesses in architecture, the patterns and textures in nature, and the rich, vibrant color and contrast all around you.

4. Then, select an object close to you. It could be architectural, such as a building or an interesting component of that building. It could be natural, such as a tree or an interesting rock outcropping. It could be man-made, such as a car or other machine. Ideally, it will be something that remains still while you examine it. As you begin exploring the object, look at it in various ways and angles. Cross your eyes, tilt your head, and even look upside-down at it if you have to, but your goal is to, extract interesting abstract patterns or textures from what you are examining.

5. Begin taking pictures at varied angles and zooms. These pictures should represent many different ways of seeing the object or merely small sections of the object. If you have the capability of taking a macro, do so and see how the object's texture changes under higher magnification. As you take pictures, step a little closer or a little further away, tilt the camera ever so slightly from one side to the other, and change the way you stand or hold the camera. Play with the available light (i.e., get the object between you and the light to take a silhouette and then get between the object and the light to snap a fully lit picture), and you could even take pictures of your shadow cast upon the object somehow. Take shots that seem like they might appeal to you, but do so without judgment of whether they are right or wrong; just keep shooting.

6. Then, locate another object nearby and repeat the same steps as before until you have about 30–40 shots in total between the two subjects.

7. Connect the device to a computer (or develop the film if doing it the old-school way), and examine each of the shots carefully. If possible, scroll through the shots in a grid format in addition to clicking through each one. Try going fast and identify what catches your eye quickest. Then, slow down and go back through them again, either front-to-back or back-to-front, with the same idea of careful, intentional selection in mind. Narrow the shots down to your top four pictures.

8. Print out the pictures and paste them into the end of this chapter as a reminder of what you will eventually take away from this brief section of the book, but also, flip forward to the pics once in a while as you make your way through, and we'll discuss this activity more later.

Okay, now go out and complete the activity before advancing further. If you skip the activity, very little of this chapter will make sense, as you need to experience the activity to truly understand, so go forth and have fun!

Did you really complete the exercise in full, or are you just peeking ahead?
If it's the latter, close the book and go do the exercise!
If the former is true, then turn the page, and let's take a closer look.

Interesting activity, isn't it? Now, equipped with your experience, let's look more closely at the intersection between mindfulness and savoring, so that we can better understand how savoring the moment can enhance our interpersonal experiences.

Enhancing Savoring with Mindful Presence

There are essentially five ways in which savoring may be enhanced or prolonged:

- **Absorption of the moment**: Allowing oneself to fully immerse into the moment being savored;
- **Sharpening the senses**: Focusing sharply, with intention and purpose, on one physical sensation while simultaneously blocking out all others to enrich the experience derived from that sensation;
- **Memory building:** The person attempting to savor the moment associates the moment with something tangible, which could include taking a photograph (as you have earlier), purchasing a souvenir, or other activities that provide a physical way to recollect for future reference;
- **Sharing:** By sharing the moment with others, the positive experience is essentially verified through a process called "symbolic interaction," which is a fundamental process of sense-making originally described by George Herbert Mead, whose theory stated that we derive meaning only out of the social interaction we have with one another while somehow employing the symbol in question. Through a process of negotiating shared meaning via communication, the experience of savoring is enriched and meaning is deepened; and
- **Self-congratulation:** Related mostly to basking, this method of enhancing savoring involves reflecting on experiences to evoke an appreciation for the set of steps leading up to successes.

Where Mindfulness and Savoring Meet

As mentioned several times previously, the nature of savoring dictates that we must invoke a purposeful present-centered awareness to enhance the savored experience. This implies the need for mindful presence to construct and maintain the savoring event, but because of the symbiotic push-pull relationship between savoring and mindful presence, savoring also tends to prolong a present-centered awareness due to a strong desire to sustain the pleasurable experience of savoring. The egg hatches into a chicken, which then in turn lays another egg, basically.

If you'll recall from way back in Chapter 1, mindfulness involves four major components to be successful: present-centered awareness, intention or purpose, an ability to distinguish novelty within the moment, and nonjudgmental acceptance of what unfolds in the moment. We've already covered how present-centered awareness affects savoring vis-a-vis the Ferris Bueller quote from above, but how do the other three interact with savoring and affect its outcomes?

Intentionality and Purpose

The idea of being in the present purposefully, with intention, sometimes has no effect on savoring, believe it or not. With certain cases of marveling, such as suddenly noticing a grand vista or a majestic sunset, the person doing the savoring is abruptly snapped away from whatever she/he was doing or thinking about previously, so in these cases, an external trigger nearly forces the person into the present-centered awareness. However, this does not mean this is an ideal case. In the camera activity, you had a set of ordered steps to undertake, and in doing so, you engaged in the activity with a clear purpose in mind. As you studied your objects and began snapping pictures from varied and diverse angles and distances, you were doing so with intention, which is one of the points of the exercise. In any other day or scenario, you likely would have walked right by the object in question, leaving its strange abstractions and textures to be discovered by another at some other time, but in seeking out the abnormal pictures, you were setting yourself up to savor by operating in the present moment on purpose, which makes savoring significantly more likely to occur.

Discovering Novelty

Perhaps the most significant contribution to savoring is the facet of mindfulness that involves the ability to derive novelty from the present moment. Being intentionally centered in the present moment without the ability to notice that which is new or unique from one moment to another is nothing more than spacing out or falling asleep with your eyes open. In fact, two forms of savoring—luxuriating and marveling—depend on external stimuli as their catalysts and cannot occur without the ability to mindfully notice details within the present moment.

During the camera exercise, this element of mindfulness was a particular highlight. Since you were specifically directed to choose an object of initial interest and then study it from multiple angles, you likely discovered wholly new ways of looking at an otherwise mundane object. This particular experience was essentially the inspiration for the title of this book, because you really are seeing something again, yet for the first time, because you are looking with curious eyes. Young children are often the most proficient at this facet of mindfulness, partly because, to them, everything really is new. There are few joys in this world more enjoyable than watching a three- to five-year-old on a mission of discovery. While their attention spans are often greatly shortened because of this tendency, every moment is amazing because every moment is fresh and new. By practicing mindfulness in our daily live and honing this ability to derive novelty from the moment, we can reconnect with that portion of our youth that tends to dissipate as we grow older and more jaded.

Nonjudgmental Acceptance

The final component of mindfulness, the ability to nonjudgmentally accept that which unfolds in the moment, can also contribute greatly to the act of savoring. Consider, for a moment, a person with more bitter or indignant nature—basically, one of those people who have a tendency to find the negative in everything and complain incessantly. Such a person, as we can easily imagine, lacks the ability to savor just about anything, and this is because such a person spends so much time judging experiences that arise that she/he fails to derive any sort of joy from those experiences. By the way, the DSM-V (the Diagnostic and Statistical Manual of psychological disorders, which is the tool used by psychologists to diagnose and treat people with mental illness) now includes bitterness as a personality disorder requiring treatment.

On the other hand, consider a gregarious person who seems to find the best in everything. Before I went into teaching and as I was finishing up my master's degree in communication studies, I worked as a human resources executive for a large national retail corporation. As part of my job, I would travel to various stores and do "walks," which was where we would assess that store's organizational health. At one store, I noticed a custodial supervisor who came in every night around closing time (the custodians for this organization work overnight while the stores are closed, locked into the store behind alarmed doors while they clean), and he was always ultra-positive and upbeat. In fact, he was so alarmingly positive that one could not help but feel like his attitude was infectious. It was like he had a natural gravitational field surrounding him that drew others closer to his vicinity, if only to pick up some positivity through osmosis. Anyway, one night, out of burning curiosity, I decided to ask him why he was always so happy. He laughed his contagious laugh and said to me:

> *Josh, every single day you see me is the best day of my life, and I'll tell you why. If I have managed to wake up again, greeted by the potential for another day in which to get things right, then I have awoken to the greatest day of my life.*

My jaw dropped to the floor. I had never heard someone share a perspective like this before. Later, as I reflected on what he said to me, I realized the truth in what he was talking about, as well as how his view is related to mindfulness. The reason he was so ready and able to savor the experiences of his life, no matter how seemingly trivial and mundane, was because he was always intentionally and consciously centered in the present, curious and open to new things, and took things as they came without suffering kneejerk reactions and judgments of those experiences. As a result, this man was not only remarkably positive and upbeat, which, again, drew others into his experience, but he also had the patience of a saint and the innovative creativity of a genius, which are additional side effects of mindfulness just beginning to be researched across the globe.

Accepting events as they unfold allows us to systematically unpack those events, looking at how each even relates to the one before it, the one after it, and the environment in which it is occurring. This provides for a more holistic understanding of various cause–effect chains of events, and with that increased understanding comes additional awareness and, of course, appreciation, which leads directly into savoring of various forms. In the end, I don't know about you, but I prefer to perceive myself more like the custodian and adopt a mindful attitude that leads to more savoring and appreciation than to be perceived as a "Debbie Downer" who embodies bitterness and wastes his time and energy complaining. We will discuss more about how our choice of how we perceive the world is a pliable characteristic in a later chapter, so stay tuned for more.

The Impact of Mindfulness and Savoring on Interaction

As stated earlier, mindfulness does not guarantee savoring experiences, but rather, cultivates savoring in much the same way that a gardener cultivates a rose. A skilled and mindful gardener tills the soil, plants the seed, feeds the soil nutrients and water, and then waits patiently while nature takes over. As the plant grows, the gardener continues to care for it until such time as the rose blossoms. In a similar fashion, we cultivate our sense of mindful presence regularly. We recognize times that are ripe for savoring and pursue even more mindful behaviors. Then, nature takes over, as savoring blossoms.

In such moments, when shared with others via mutual interaction, remarkable and miraculous things can happen to those relationships. One of the most memorable interactions between my wife and I occurred in 2012. It was a weekend day, and we were trapped inside because of the typical Pacific Northwest spring rain that never seems to end. As a result, we were going a bit stir crazy, and when that happens, emotions tend to run a bit hot, and we all have more of a tendency to get on one another's nerves, whether it's her and I or the kids. Anyway, my wife started yelling at the kids a bit disproportionately, even for an irritable rainy day. We had started cleaning the house, and the more she cleaned and discovered, the more irritable she became, and the yelling not only became more frequent, but took on a much darker, ominous tone. I started to worry as I saw the hurt look on my kids' faces, but they stayed quiet (wise choice, guys) and kept cleaning. I, in all my infinite wisdom (that's sarcasm, by the way), spoke up and mentioned to my wife that maybe she was being a little harsh on the kids. That, my friends, was gasoline on an already-blazing bonfire. Suddenly, I was the recipient of her yelling, which was even more tense. Normally, I would have snapped back at her, and we probably would have fought on and on for a good couple of hours, but there was something about this situation that struck me differently; something about it caused me to realize that she needed me to be mindful and present in this moment.

So, I walked up to her, took her hand, which she tried pulling away, mumbling, "Don't touch me!" I gently pulled her to the couch and asked her to sit with me. "I don't want to sit!" she snapped angrily. I insisted that she just take a seat for a moment, imploring her as calmly as possible to take a sort of time-out with me. She slumped into the couch, using all of her nonverbal signals to reassure me that everything was so not okay.

I placed my hand on her knee softly, at which she glared, then I looked into her eyes and said, "What's wrong?"

"Why does something have to be wrong," she snapped again, "Can't you just let me have a bad day?"

"Normally," I began, "yes, but this is different somehow." I became even more mindful of my tone, ensuring that what I said next effectively expressed my sincere concern, "*Something* is wrong, and I want you to talk to me. I'm worried about you."

At that, she paused, and within seconds, tears were streaming down her face (and my wife is so not a crier). The tears gave way to sobs, and I put my arm around her, pulling her in and placing her head on my chest. As she sobbed uncontrollably, she lamented about her grandmother, who was being moved from advanced care to hospice, knowing that the end of her life was imminent. Her grandmother was practically a saint and acted as the matriarch of my wife's gargantuan Scandinavian family, not to mention one of the kindest, gentlest, most compassionate humans I have ever had the honor and pleasure of knowing, so to state that this news was difficult for her to take is a dramatic understatement. As my wife's core issue unraveled, I recognized the need to be even more mindful than usual, because it was my presence and the gift of listening that was affording her the opportunity to open up and unload.

See, her anger prior to this interaction was merely a symptom, as anger usually is. Anger is a secondary emotion—a mask we wear when we are unable to productively and healthily cope with difficult emotions—in her case, grief and worry. Without being mindful enough to recognize this, not only would I not have helped her work through these emotions and cope with an incredibly difficult time in her life, I would have fanned the flames and exasperated a painful situation by unnecessarily fighting with her over something so incredibly insignificant.

Once she finished articulating her worry and grief, with me listening mindfully (giving her the necessary space to open up without judgment or attempting to "fix" her issues), the anger disappeared. She thanked me sincerely for providing the gift of listening and then went to sit down and apologize to our children one at a time, explaining the grave nature of the situation to each of them. Through my mindful presence, I not only helped her work her way through anger, grief, and worry, but I helped her become more mindful and calm as well, which she then demonstrated in her request for forgiveness from our children for her earlier actions. Even more to the point, she was able to be mindfully present for the kids, as she broke the news of her grandmother to them.

Throughout this whole interaction, I found myself experiencing the thanksgiving form of savoring, as the lesson of mindful presence was a gift I had learned elsewhere and was exceedingly grateful to have used in such a generative way. Like I mentioned, any other day, I would have simply blindly fought with my wife over something stupid, but the powerful moral of this story is to consciously watch for situations in which mindfulness is the best course of action, a principle closely related to the quote at the beginning of this chapter (go ahead, look at it one more time really quick). Also, one of the lessons we will explore later is how taking action ourselves can pave the way for others as well, whether through mirroring our actions or reciprocating them, and this is how one becomes a strong interpersonal leader.

Activity 2: Everyday Vacation

This is the only chapter that has two activities, but it's because the principles buried within them are important enough to reinforce twice. This particular activity is one that I recommend doing daily for at least one week—seven days in a row without fail. After that, you can decide whether you no longer want to do it, but I suspect it will become a regular part of your routine:

1. Each and every day, plan for and complete a "daily vacation" in which you spend at least 20 minutes doing something you personally find enjoyable, but one major rule you have to follow is that this activity cannot involve a screen (no phone games, no video games, no TV, no movies, no YouTube, no social media). Consider gardening, reading, going out for a cup of coffee or ice cream, visiting a museum, take a long soaking bath, hang out with a friend, or take a walk. You may even consider using one of the activities from Chapter 2 (i.e., Walks to Nowhere, Last Supper, etc.). You do not have to do the same activity every single day, but you should at the very least set aside the same amount of time each day to take a vacation from your regularly scheduled life;

2. Before you embark on this personal daily vacation, use the pages at the end of this chapter to log your worries, stresses, responsibilities, and concerns that you are currently experiencing. Don't spend too much time and detail; highlights will suffice;

3. While on this personal vacation, take time to intentionally notice any and all aspects of the activity that give you some form of pleasure. Actively identify what the positive feeling is that arises, and then build a memory of both the feeling and the aspect of the activity you associated with that feeling. For example, if I decide to take a walk to nowhere, and I notice that I suddenly feel stress-free and relaxed, then I think about how good such walks are for me, between the physical activity and the stress-reduction aspect. Another example could be if I take a time-out to leave the house and go take pictures of the sunset, during which I might experience a sense of awe, which I associate with the grandeur of the moment. As you identify each feeling and associated aspect, imagine yourself swishing the feeling around in your mind for a few moments like one might swish a fine wine around when tasting it;

4. Once your personal vacation is complete, the next immediate thing you should do is plan your vacation for the next day. Decide what you are going to do, commit to a time, put the time in your phone as a reminder, and then look forward to that activity;
5. At the end of the day, before going to bed, think back to that day's activity. Allow yourself to remember the feelings you experienced and do so with fondness. Set a reminder in your phone to do this, if needed; and
6. Lastly, at the conclusion of the seven-day period, take time to look back through the personal vacations you took over the course of the week. Try to recall what pleasurable feelings arose in each one and what aspects of the activities facilitated those feelings. Then, compare how you feel at the end of the week with how you normally feel at the end of the week and consider the reflection questions below.

Questions for Reflection

- Were you happier by the end of the week? Were you happier during the week as well?
- How did writing down your concerns and worries affect the way you experienced your personal vacations? Do you think it was a way of "bookmarking" your spot so that you didn't need to carry those with you while on vacation? What can you take away from this for everyday use?
- What did the process of mindfully noticing your feelings as they arose do for your experience of those feelings?
- How did immediately planning your next personal vacation generate anticipation? What role does anticipation play in savoring?
- How did recollection and reminiscence of your vacations affect you? What role does reminiscing play in the art of savoring the moment?

Daily Worry Log for Everyday Vacations

Day 1

_____
_____
_____
_____
_____
_____
_____

Day 2

_____
_____
_____

Day 3

Day 4

Day 5

Day 6

Day 7

CHAPTER 11

Cultivating Gratitude

It is possible to live happily in the here and now. So many conditions of happiness are available—more than enough for you to be happy right now. You don't have to run into the future in order to get more.

—Thich Nhat Hanh

At first glance, we could easily assume savoring and appreciation or gratitude are essentially the same. After all, as we savor, we immerse ourselves into the pleasure of appreciation, whether it is being grateful for earning a raise at work, eating a delicious meal, or noticing a beautiful sunrise over the ocean. However, gratitude, appreciation, and savoring are subtly different concepts, even though they are closely interrelated, and the purpose of this chapter is to begin exploring those nuances and applying them to our interpersonal relationships.

Activity: Gratitude Journal

As with the last chapter, **this chapter's activity absolutely must begin right away** so that you *feel* the concepts we are exploring throughout not only this chapter, but subsequent chapters as well. Without experiencing the full effects of appreciation, it would be extraordinarily difficult to discuss the many effects that gratitude has on our interpersonal relationships.

Starting as soon as you read this, each and every day for the next six weeks, use the margins of this book to write down five things that you are grateful for in that moment, and complete this activity as soon as possible after waking up (or whenever you begin your day, if you work an overnight job). Date each set of five things you are grateful for so that you can easily trace your way back through the list later on, as you will need to avoid repeating any one item over the course of the activity (therein lies the challenge). Set an alarm or reminder in your phone if necessary to keep yourself honest and on track. It is *absolutely critical* that you make this a consistently daily habit—as you start your day—for it to have the desired effect for the purposes of our exploration of the impact of gratitude.

This exercise is challenging, but not impossible. Generally, people start this activity with more general gratitude, such as, "I'm grateful for: 1) sunny days, 2) my dog, 3) my loving partner, 4) chocolate, and 5) coffee." Writing a list like this does not mean that you cannot later be grateful for those same five things; it simply requires you to more carefully articulate what it is about those things toward which you feel most grateful. For example, in a later entry, that same person could write: "I'm grateful for: 1) the warm feeling of the sun's rays on my back, 2) the way my dog wakes me up with kisses, 3) the way my partner accepts me unconditionally, 4) chocolate-covered peanut butter, and 5) the aroma of coffee flooding my kitchen in the morning." Also, the items for which you are grateful need not be profound or poetic. One day, you might look around and feel grateful for sticky notes, staplers, paper clips, a three-hole punch, and multicolored highlighters (no offense intended to fans of office supplies). If you feel a genuine sense of gratitude for those items, write them down, by all means!

As you can imagine, as the exercise progresses, you are somewhat "forced" to better articulate specifically what inspires a sense of gratitude for you. If you do this every day for six weeks without fail, you will have over 200 items to be grateful for, a list full of reminders of why life is good. If you miss a day, that's okay. Like a medical doctor tells you with antibiotics, simply try to catch up as soon as possible. In fact, think of this activity sort of as an antibiotic for life; you will be amazed at how much "better" you start feeling in a relatively short period of time. However, that doesn't necessarily mean that this activity is all rainbows, unicorns, and fluffy mewing kittens all the time. There likely will be points in this exercise where it has the potential to take a darker turn. During the process of awakening gratitude, we can at times compare our new grateful perspective with our old perspective of taking life for granted, and, in turn, this inspires feelings of guilt or remorse for not having been more grateful in the past. If this occurs, simply notice and acknowledge the feeling, but then let it pass without latching onto it and ruminating. Again, the key is not in quality (so don't judge your choices); rather, it is in consistency. Do this every day for six weeks, at the start of your day, and try not to repeat items. Start in the margins of this page—when the page is too full to write any more, go back to the previous page, etc. Perhaps you can fill the margins of this book with items for which you are grateful, but try not to cover up the writing, as you may wish to come back and re-read some of these passages.

Of Gratitude and Perception

The optimist says the glass is half-full. The pessimist says the glass is half-empty. The realist says the glass has a 1:1 ratio of air to liquid. The opportunist drinks it down, laughs at the others' inaction, and says, "Better luck next time."

Learning to appreciate the best of life is what positive psychologists call an "attitude of gratitude," which is much more than merely a catchy rhyme—it is a way of life. As you explore this chapter, speculate on how your life might be different by learning to find the silver lining in even the worst of things. As you do this, contemplate the following quote by Viktor Frankl: "Everything can be taken from a [hu]man but one thing: the last of the human freedoms—to choose one's attitude in any given set of circumstances, to choose one's own way."

Viktor Frankl was a survivor of one of history's darkest tragedies: the Nazi holocaust. As he struggled to stay alive and hold on to hope during his ordeals throughout several of the most notorious death camps, Frankl realized that those around him who were dying all had something in common: They had lost hope and subsequently possessed no reason left to live. It was amid the darkest depths of despair and as he faced certain death that Frankl's life was changed through the realization that, if humans can find meaning in even the most hopeless situations, then we can find a way through. He later used his imagination to envision meeting his wife again after the war as a way to survive his experience in the camps until they were liberated, and then he went on to found what has been called the third major Viennese school of psychology (logotherapy), the first two of which were credited to Sigmund Freud (psychoanalysis) and Alfred Adler (individual psychology).

Ultimately, we have the capability to shape our perceptions based on how we frame our interpretation of the world around us. A well-known saying suggests that, "To the child with a hammer, everything looks like a nail." For example, a child with nothing to do will randomly look around for some form of entertainment or activity to occupy her/his mind. The moment that child picks up a hammer, the child's brain becomes focused on the intended purpose of the hammer, which of course is to strike things, and suddenly, the child no longer looks at things the same way. An empty glass bottle on the curb may have been benign litter that went without notice before possession of the hammer, but after clutching the tool and having potential to destroy it, the bottle represents something to be shattered for the sake of entertainment (and this is how many children get into mischief—adults, too).

The same is true of our everyday lives. To a pessimist or someone suffering chronic bitterness, everything is worthy of complaint. The newest blockbuster sci-fi movie, to a pessimist like this, is viewed with cynicism and harsh critique, as they notice only that which is deserving of critique. They will nit-pick their experiences apart with ridiculous detail, framing their perceptions of their life experiences as negative. Why some people do this is another book chapter for another topic area, as it falls more into the domain of psychology, but what we can examine is how to alter such perceptions.

If a pessimist is someone who walks around with a critique-hammer, looking for things to destroy for themselves and others, then how can we consciously make a decision to change such behavior? The key word here is a fun one to say: perturbation. To perturb something is to cause a systemic deviation by adding an outside influence to throw the entire system off its usual course. In other words, it's the wrench in the machine. Behavior, like physical motion, can possess momentum, and the stronger the momentum, the more difficult it will be to perturb the system. For example, if someone has been a pessimist ever since a traumatic event that occurred over 20 years ago, then that person cannot simply wake up one day, make a change, and expect it to make wide, sweeping, systematic alterations to that person's behavior. Such perturbations require not only the initial shock to the system, but prolonged and sustained alteration to take effect.

Such is the potential power of gratitude. Using tools like the gratitude list prescribed as the activity for this chapter (you are remembering to do it every day, as you start your day, right?), we can slowly make systematic changes to our behaviors, and often times, those changes happen so subtly that we don't notice they've radically changed us for the better until well after the fact. While it doesn't seem like a list of five things presents the potential to make that huge of a difference, the results of such an activity speak for themselves. However, those results can vary a bit from week to week.

Expect Week 1 to be filled with simply getting into the habit and trying not to repeat any of the more obvious items for which to be grateful.

During Week 2, the habit has generally solidified, and you might find yourself collecting items for which to be grateful later. For example, if you are playing by the rules and have written down five thoughtful things for which to be grateful at the start of your day, then as the day goes on, you may likely begin noticing items that would make great material for your list the next day, committing them to memory to give you a jump start on the list for the next morning.

By Week 3, the list has become a regular part of your routine, and you may feel a sense of anticipation for the moment when you write down items for which you are grateful. You may likely continue collecting items to use throughout your day, but you will also find that there are too many items to remember, leaving you with the opposite problem of not necessarily having too few items to write, but too many from which to choose.

During Week 4, people generally start refining the way they articulate their selections and noticing the differences between mindful gratitude and backhanded gratitude. Mindful gratitude (i.e., "I am grateful that I can find wisdom in even the toughest life lessons") is genuine and concentrates on the positive, while backhanded gratitude is often riddled with implied insults or complaints conveniently wrapped in a gratitude blanket (i.e., "I am so grateful that my horrible monster of an ex is no longer in my life"). The question arises, can backhanded gratitude really fulfill the function of expressing appreciation? In my opinion, I would say that, no, they don't, as the ratio of gratitude to complaint is probably too small to matter. It's like a juice pouch—you're lucky if the "juice" contains 10% real fruit juice. The rest is filler. So, watch out for these, and don't allow your gratitude list to gradually transform into a complaint list.

Around Week 5 and Week 6, depending on the person, you will begin to slowly realize the radical change that has occurred, but you will not be able to put your finger on exactly when it happened. I don't want to spoil the ending for you, but suffice it to say that, providing you do this regularly, each and every day at the start of your day, you will likely undergo a complete perception shift. Events will appear differently, as you will have a full, life-affirming list of the things that make existence worthwhile occupying the space formerly taken up by a hammer, and instead of searching for things to proverbially hit with that hammer, you will become a collector of all things good.

Back when I was a doctoral student, I shared several classes with a Filipino Catholic priest we lovingly called Jim (I think he chose that nickname, since his given name was much longer and more difficult to pronounce). He was a quiet fellow who rarely spoke up in class, and I think most of us simply assumed that, because he was an English as a Second Language (ESL) student, he was too nervous, self-conscious, or shy to speak up. But that was before we all got to know him. See, Jim was not quiet because he felt he had to be quiet; Jim was quiet because he chose to be silent. Jim was listening, and while he took everything in, he slowly and deliberately shaped his contribution to our discussions to ensure they were of the highest possible quality. In a 16-week semester-long class, I think we heard Jim speak up in class discussions three or four times, so whenever he did speak up, everyone would listen.

One day, we were having a class discussion on cultivating an attitude of gratitude, and our group's conversation was electric. Our discussion moved so fast that we could barely get our thoughts out in turn before the conversation took yet another detour. Everyone but Jim contributed. Our professor noticed, and she shushed us as a group, inviting him to speak, "Jim, what do you think?" I'll never forget his reaction. He seemed so genuinely pleased to have someone call on him and deliberately ask his opinion, but he didn't answer right away. Instead, he leaned back, arching his back on the desk's back rest before his head soon followed until he was looking up at the ceiling. After a cat-like stretch that seemed like an eternity, Jim took a deep and intentional breath before he began—the suspense was terrible. Then, he opened his mouth and said one of the most profoundly memorable things I had ever heard a peer utter:

> *How odd is it that we don't appreciate our health until we are sick? And how odd is it that we do not take notice of the very breath that keeps us alive until running up a flight of stairs threatens to take it from us? Oh, the good it would do us to learn to appreciate the many miracles of life before they are gone!*

Jim was absolutely right. As I left the class that day, I recall walking outside and suddenly noticing the crisp, spring air. The colors all around me seemed more intense and vivid, and the long freeway drive back home took a little longer, partly because I didn't feel as rushed as normal. It was like Jim's one comment that day was my perturbance, snapping me out of my rut of thinking and behaving and causing me to suddenly notice more. It was as if his comment made me look at the proverbial hammer in my own hand, before dropping it completely.

Alan Uster / Shutterstock.com

Gratitude opens us up to the abundance of life happening all around us. As we begin to focus on that for which we are grateful, we start to see the source of that gratitude, opening us up to the complex web of interconnection existing all around us. Not only does gratitude cause us to recognize the good we receive from others, but it also motivates us to do good for others and strengthens our resolve to continue doing good in the future. Gratitude creates and sustains a more optimistic attitude by perturbing and sometimes all together stopping the momentum of negative thought patterns. Gratitude is a game changer, but must be felt and experienced to be understood, so get going on those daily lists, and notice what changes you feel in the upcoming weeks.

You won't regret it.

CHAPTER 12

Appreciation—The Outward Expression of Gratitude

The deepest principle of human nature is a craving to be appreciated.

—William James

In the last chapter, we explored the impact that gratitude has on us, personally. In this chapter, we put our newfound gratitude practice to the test by expanding it to others, where we will examine the impact that the expression of gratitude, or the sharing of it with others by way of communicating appreciation, can have upon our everyday interactions. After all, a gratitude practice is pretty selfish if we are the only ones affected by doing so.

To start, I'll share a story, this time from my brief experience as a human resources executive. Back then, my immediate boss was not the warm-fuzzy-touchy type who engaged much in people- or team-building, but one day, he decided to shake things up and try something out of the blue. He called together everyone in the organization (about 30 people or so, and we gathered together, almost naturally forming a circle, at the apex of which was my boss). He then proceeded to tell us he was going to try something unusual and start our work day off with a round of thank-yous. We would go around the circle, and each person would thank someone else in the room, verbally and in front of the whole group. He went first and thanked me, despite our sometimes-rocky relationship (for some reason, I was able to push his buttons better than most others). I remember feeling a little awkward, but at the same time, my heart swelled as he thanked me. I vividly recall the feeling, even as I type this out, although I have long forgotten for what he specifically thanked me. We then went around the circle, and as more and more people vocalized their appreciation for others, I noticed something interesting happen to the otherwise sour Monday-morning mood most of us packed around with us like luggage: It disappeared. Its place arose a sort of jovial, collegial atmosphere, and the awkward silence was replaced by smiles and laughter.

Later, my boss and I instituted a system of formal thank-yous that were written on little business cards he had printed up, and those cards would then be displayed for all to see, before going into a drawing for a lavish prize once a month. What we found, however, was that people seemed less motivated by the prizes and more by the general feelings of goodness being created, both by giving thanks as well as receiving public admiration from others. Within a month, the general mood within the organization had a noticeably positive vibe to it, human resource issues and complaints were measurably down from before, and people were motivated intrinsically to do better all-around work. This all happened with a 15-minute morning activity and about $50 in custom business cards!

The expression of gratitude—*appreciation*—carries with it very real and tangible effects. It may seem like a complete no-brainer to say that people like to feel valued and appreciated, but what does the research say? First of all, people who feel valued tend to also have significantly more positive or optimistic attitudes, which leads in part to increasing the likelihood of intrinsic motivation, or the act of doing something right to achieve a certain sense of self-satisfaction, rather than doing it well to elicit praise and respect from others. This one seems pretty easy to follow; if we work hard on behalf of someone else, and that person fails to show any appreciation or at least an appropriate level of appreciation for our work, then what is the likelihood of us providing those efforts again? Expressing appreciation motivates others and keeps them in a positive relationship with those who express it.

Second, not only do those on the receiving end of appreciation feel better and maintain more positive attitudes, but when we are the givers of such appreciation, we receive benefits from the act as well. People who show appreciation for others enjoy many physical and emotional benefits, such as better sleep, greater emotional resilience, higher optimism, and relational satisfaction. On a more selfish level, providing more appreciation for others earns us greater social capital, which is the gravity that draws others toward us by making us more attractive (and not only in a physical sense of the word).

Third, the expression of appreciation taps into something deep within our psyches. As we express our gratitude thoughtfully and with intention, it activates the mirror neurons of the person on the receiving end, while simultaneously activating the reward hormones within the brain, such as dopamine and serotonin. Not only does this act make others feel good, but it activates the process of reciprocity. Most people will reciprocate gratitude as they receive it, creating a two-way exchange of positive emotion that completes the cycle and arouses those same emotions in the original expresser of appreciation, as that person then becomes the recipient of the reciprocated gratitude.

Fourth, when applied to relationships, the expression of appreciation can supercharge that relationship like few other behaviors. People who express their appreciation for romantic partners not only tend to forgive others quicker and more fully, but also tend to be considerably less narcissistic as they turn their focus outward and away from themselves. Providing thanks to others where the emotion is genuinely felt can strengthen relationship bonds while encouraging relationship maintenance, as well as satisfaction and a deeper feeling of connection.

Activity: Priming a Grateful Interaction

For this chapter's activity, you are putting the data on appreciation previously outlined to the test. To begin, choose one day in your gratitude journal right away to focus on writing down what you are grateful for with respect to only one person. Write down five (or more) things you are thankful for in that person, and be specific. Once you have this list, reflect on various situations where you feel like that person has exemplified these traits for which you are grateful. Then, later in the *same day*, contact that person, preferably in-person if possible, and have a conversation with that person about anything that comes to mind (you are not talking about the gratitude list during this conversation—make it a "normal" conversation with this person). Do it as sincerely and genuinely as possible, and pay close attention to the outcome of this interaction. Afterward, consider the following questions before reading further. Did you end up being surprised at the way the interaction felt, or did you see it coming? Have you ever had a similar feel to an interaction like this before, and if so, what prompted it? What do you think would happen if you did this on a regular basis with those you care about?

Using Appreciation to Reframe Interaction

If you are like most of my students who have done this activity in the past, then you probably enjoyed your interaction immensely. I've often heard students say that they had no intention of taking the interaction as far as it ended up going, but that they talked into the wee hours of the late night or early morning. Conversations lasting four or more hours as a result of this exercise are not all that uncommon, but the question this activity begs is, why?

The answer lies in the concept of reframing, which is the idea that we can consciously and intentionally draw our own frame around an interaction before entering into that conversation, and we can do so with the expressed purpose of altering the outcome. We can also think of this as putting on a different pair of glasses to see differently for conversations with diverse groups of people. For example, if I knew I had to argue with a salesperson about a refund, I might reframe my attitude heading into the conversation to be more of a shrewd negotiator. That same reframing, of course, will not work when trying to convince my children to do their chores, and as a result, I reframe my perceptions differently heading into such interactions.

In this instance, by consciously choosing gratitude as the catalyst for our reframing, we used the expression of appreciation to prime our perceptions of those with whom we chose to interact for the sake of the activity. As we considered at least five areas for which to be grateful, followed by a short reflection, we softened our approach to that person and evoked many of the principles discussed earlier in the chapter, such as self-motivation, optimism, and an all-around more positive attitude before heading into the conversation.

All of this is intricately interconnected with our other focus areas for Part 3 of this book, effectively tying together mindfulness, savoring, gratitude, and appreciation. We begin by placing ourselves into a mindful state, where we stop, take a look around, and deliberately and intentionally act with purpose. As we do so, we invoke the act of savoring, whether through savoring our current states or doing so with either anticipation (future savoring) or reminiscence (savoring the past). This, in turn, invokes gratitude, and as our gratefulness builds up, we seek methods to express our appreciation with the sole purpose of sharing it with others. Woven together, these four concepts present us with a roadmap to greater physical, emotional, and mental health for ourselves, as well as significantly greater relational health as applied to our interactions with others. Taken together as a related system or total package, mindfulness, savoring, gratitude, and appreciation can be used intentionally, rather than simply wandering from one experience to another, all while hoping such experiences result in one or more of these four life-affirming characteristics. We can better control our behaviors such that we recognize moments where we need to be more present through mindfulness, moments we know for a fact are worth slowing down to savor, moments where gratitude can only augment our experiences, and moments where we ought to express appreciation for others' contributions to those experiences. And who doesn't want these benefits? I think I speak for all, if not at least most of us, when I state that being able to utilize these characteristics on a moment's notice will help us get much more out of our life's experiences.

To illustrate this, I'd like to share a brief story from one of my own experiences where these characteristics were employed successfully. For the most part, it started out just like any other mid-September weekend. Still shorts weather, there was nary a cloud in the sky, oodles of sunshine, and still a bit of warmth, save for the subtle pre-autumn bite. We didn't have much in the way of plans for the weekend, save for a visit to the fair on Sunday for our annual and highly anticipated consumption of life-shortening fried fare, testing abdominal stamina by way of a few thrill rides, and testing our mettle by pushing ourselves beyond our comfort zones with a few trips down a zip line.

The day before this outing, we all got together for a mostly unplanned family dinner at Grandma's house, and in all honesty, this Saturday was not all that remarkable compared to any other mid-September day. My wife and her family conversed on the other side of the front room after we had just finished a generous helping of one of my mother-in-law's soul food offerings: sausage–potato casserole. There was a familiar sense of joy in the air, the kind of latent happiness one feels on Christmas Day in the gentle lull between opening presents and preparing dinner. The room was filled with the kind of aura that makes a smile feel effortless.

Just as I noticed this feeling wash over me, I turned my attention to the front room window. My two youngest kids had just gone outside to play in the front yard, and I saw them hop up and over the tailgate to my father-in-law's truck, where they started jumping up and down, making the truck bounce slightly. At that moment, it felt as though I had entered a time warp and was peering through a hazy mist at my own childhood memories.

Courtesy Josh Misner.

The year was probably around 1985 or 1986, but I couldn't say for sure, since concrete details such as dates, times, and exact places are trivial and meaningless in those among our most formative childhood memories. What really counts are the experiences we share with the best of friends, such as jumping off a tailgate just to be able to dunk a miniature basketball and pretend we were Air Jordan, or trying to hit a whiffle ball hard enough to force our best friends have to knock on the cranky old neighbor's door to gain access to his backyard so it could be retrieved.

This is not wistful reminiscing or digging up old memories as a way to dodge the oft-complex difficulties of the present. These are memories of the power and glory of our youth. These were likely some of the greatest days of our lives, back before the weight of the world shifted to our shoulders, which, at times, can easily rob us of our imagination.

As I watched my kids play with their cousin outside in the driveway, a realization hit me like a gut punch, and in a very literal sense, it took my breath away as I realized what I was watching. These were *their* glory days. These were the greatest times of *their* lives, and I consider it a gift—*an absolute miracle*—to have had a front-row seat for these moments. Seeing them play at that moment is now a memory I still savor, having filled me with gratitude and joy, but it also altered my perspective by begging the following questions:

What if I was mindful enough to be able to recognize these moments, as they happen?

What if I could recognize when their proverbial memory cameras are rolling, collecting footage that they will later replay in reminiscence, once they are adults, and then step into the frame, so that I might become an important character within those moments?

This is the essence of being mindful: To recognize the moments when we, our presence is needed most and to have the initiative to step in and play a significant role as necessary. Such is also the essence of savoring, gratitude, and the subsequent expression of appreciation. Once mindfulness creates the foundation for us to stop, look around, and recognize the subtle power in such moments, it lays the groundwork for everything else to begin.

Revisiting Our "Issues"

To wrap up Part 3 of this book, we need to dig up the past a bit. Go back to the activity at the end of Chapter 8, which guided you to select one of the areas for improvement derived from your communication audit at the end of Chapter 4. When we last saw this issue, we were wrestling with accountability and agonizing over the vulnerability that invoked. This time, we look through a positive psychology lens at this same issue. Below, using the space provided, I want you to write a reflection on the impact that the four-pronged positive psychology approach—mindfulness, savoring, gratitude, and the expression of appreciation—might have on your interpersonal relationships in general, as well as they might help you address the issue you identified at the end of Chapter 8. How might the gratitude journal activity (you're still doing it every day, right?) shape your perceptions as you continue to approach and resolve this issue? How will your knowledge of these characteristics affect future interactions surrounding the issue you chose to address?

For example, in Chapter 8, I mentioned social media addiction as a potential issue to address, and I concluded that awareness of such an addiction and how it impacts others would be a great place to start addressing this condition. At this point, I would probably discuss how becoming more mindful of when I succumb to such an addiction and how it affects my relationships. Then, I would look at how, as I reduce my tendency to mindlessly check in on social media, I will increase my availability with others and subsequently also increase the likelihood of finding moments to savor. I could then use my imagination to articulate how such moments would make me feel grateful for having set aside my device to become more present, but more than that, I could speculate on how mindfully doing so would likely result in garnering the appreciation of others for being more mindfully aware, which would also make me more likely to express my appreciation for having been a party to such encounters. Do your best to articulate this as fully as possible, as it will become a building block for the ultimate goal at the end of this book.

Notes

PART 4 Connecting

In the final four-chapter part of our journey through this book, we will weave together the previous three parts of the book as a means to explore connection with others using mindfulness as our common thread. Initially, we will look at how gratitude fosters humility. Once we recognize the relational benefits of humility, we will examine a specific philosophy of interaction that hails from leadership studies as a roadmap for stronger relationships. Third, borrowing from organizational theory, we will use an organizational theory to examine how to further refine our perceptions and alter the way we view relational issues for the better. Lastly, we will tie everything together and develop a sustainable long-term strategy for employing the concepts of this book to whatever issue(s) you chose to explore further (see chapters 4, 8, and 12).

Our goals during this fourth and final part of the book are as follows:

- Identify methods to transform appreciation into humility
- Articulate a personal leadership philosophy with respect to relationships
- Define the method of appreciative inquiry as it applies to interpersonal connection
- Develop a strategy for utilizing and sustaining restorative interpersonal communication beyond the conclusion of this book

CHAPTER 13

Linking Humility with Gratitude

Humility is throwing oneself away in complete concentration on something or someone else.
—Madeleine L'Engle

While chapter 11 introduced us to the wonders of gratitude on the soul, and chapter 12 explored how the expression of gratitude through appreciation is great for our relationships, we are now going to take this even further by looking specifically at the act of expressing appreciation through the lens of vulnerability. Yes, that soul-crushing concept from chapter 8 has returned, but remember that I mentioned we were intentionally tying together the many aspects already examined throughout this book, so don't think I didn't warn you.

What is humility, exactly, and furthermore, why study it? Most definitions of humility mention that it involves lowering one's importance in relation to others, or is the process of de-emphasizing one's status in favor of exalting another. Gandhi stated that attempts to discover truth without humility are doomed to become an "arrogant caricature" of truth. Confucius suggested that humility was "the solid foundation of all virtues." Leadership studies across the globe are currently prescribing methods for leaders to attain greater humility (quite the paradox) as a means to become more approachable and authentic. Critics often suggest that humility is actually a weakness, though more recent studies are discovering that it is quite the opposite, as there is an important distinction to make between humiliation and being humble. Humiliation is giving in to the will of others and allowing oneself to be dominated, whereas acting humbly is a measure of strength demonstrated through accountability, personal responsibility, and honesty. People adopting humble attitudes have been shown to cope better with anxiety (i.e., resilience), have higher self-control (the opposite of which, people who are obsessed with themselves, tend to act more out of self-interest), experience lower levels of prejudice, are more helpful, and experience greater relational satisfaction. In fact, humble people sound like significantly happier, well-adjusted, and all-around good people.

So, why us and why now? Well, a funny thing happens to us when we approach someone for whom we care deeply and genuinely and sincerely express our appreciation for something that person embodies. To effectively express such appreciation, we must lower ourselves while we place the other person on a proverbial pedestal, a process that requires not only for us to make ourselves vulnerable, but to express ourselves with humility. Before we move forward, I ask that you complete this chapter's activity, again as a measure of *feeling* what we are discussing later for better understanding.

Activity: Humble Appreciation

Looking back at what you have written in your gratitude list up to this point (you *are* still writing that in the margins every day at the start of your day, right?), select something you are grateful for that is closely connected to another person. For example, if I wrote in my gratitude list one day that I am grateful to feel loved by someone whom I also love deeply, then I might choose someone who makes me feel most loved. Or, if I wrote that I am grateful for bluntly honest critique, then I might choose the realist in my life (my wife) to express my appreciation for her ability to call me out if I ever act arrogant or like a know-it-all. Yet another, slightly more surface-level example might be that, if I am grateful for well-made coffee, I might select my favorite barista to use for the activity. Once you have chosen both the quality for which you already expressed gratitude in your list, as well as the person who embodies that quality in your life, then if possible, meet with that person face-to-face, and express your appreciation for that person's ability to exemplify the trait you are grateful for.

To do this will require a certain level of humility on your part, as your task will be to elevate another person on a genuine and authentic level, so take careful note of the level of humility required for you to openly express that appreciation and elevate the other. The level of humility will vary depending on your relationship with the person you chose to express appreciation for, as well as the topic area being discussed. Obviously, if I am going to thank my barista for the wonderful job she does in making my coffee, I'm probably not going to need to evoke a terribly high level of humility, as compared to expressing gratitude to my boss for the way she critiqued me during her last evaluation of my work performance. Choose wisely, but at the same time, challenge yourself and maybe even repeat the activity on multiple people, taking note of the various levels of humility you experience. Then, come back to this part, and read further into why humility is a necessary component of our relationships if we desire stronger connections with others.

Analyzing the Benefits and Use of Humility

Now that you have some fresh experience under your belt with respect to actually feeling humility, how did it go? If you're anything like hundreds of my prior students embarking on this exercise, then you may have noticed a few things happen during the activity. First, you probably grew a little anxious heading into it. That anxiety, however, was less like pre-speech anxiety (a.k.a., terror) and more like pre-roller coaster anxiety (a.k.a., anticipation). We can predictably and safely assume that the expression of appreciation with someone is not going to result in conflict, so our pre-expression anxiety is relatively tame in comparison with public speaking. Those feelings of anxiety, however, are those which prime us for humility, for they put us under emotional strain. In the same manner that the emotion of courage is easier to assess during situations involving personal threat, humility is easier to assess during moments where defensiveness is a potential outcome. Now, even though I mentioned just a moment ago that a defensive reaction is highly unlikely, that's not how we interpret this scenario initially. As we approach the person, ready to express appreciation, there is always that latent fear in the backs of our minds that suggests that other person is going to think we are insanely stupid for appreciating something so trivial, and that is where vulnerability comes into play. So, as we make ourselves vulnerable in the off chance that someone might ridicule us, we also notice as we make ourselves smaller in relation to the other person.

Second, you may have noticed the other person reciprocating. Even if your expression of gratitude for the other person is so highly tailored and specific that there is no way the other person could possibly say thank-you in return, there are still ways that others will find to do just that. It's almost as if it is a natural reaction (hint: It is, through mirror neurons). In fact, this habit is so deeply ingrained in me to say, "To you as well" in response to someone thanking me that, within the last few years, I've even taken to saying it after someone wishes me a happy birthday. Imagine that awkward conversation for a moment: "Happy birthday, Josh!" . . . "You too . . . er, I mean, uh, never mind."

Next, think about the following principle: It is easier to recognize humility in others than in ourselves. In most cases, our behaviors related to interpersonal assessments, such as humility, kindness, generosity, or listening ability, are assessed best by others telling us how we are doing. This is why we had the incredibly uncomfortable exercise back in chapter 3. Most of us tend to be pretty horrible at accurately assessing ourselves when it comes to our interpersonal performance. Now, intrapersonal characteristics are something we calculate pretty well, such as our attitudes, beliefs, or opinions.

If humility is easier for us to recognize in others, then let's think about the humblest person we all know. Take a moment to identify this person and then proceed when ready. Got it? Good, okay, when we think about such a person, and how it feels to interact with her or him, what is it like? For me, when it comes to being around someone humble, I am suddenly put at ease. I feel like I could tell that person anything, and it would be okay. It's almost as though something inside of me simply lets go, and I am suddenly the real, authentic me. With a person who radiates humility, we feel at ease because we know we will be accepted as we are. There is something gentle and compassionate about humility when we see it in others.

When we realize that a humble person is in our presence, we also realize that this person does not look at us as a salary, a job title, another pretty face, etc., but rather, that person recognizes the intrinsic value we have as human beings. We are seen as meaningful to someone who radiates humility, not because of shallow, physical worth and what we can offer that person in return, but because that person values us for the potential relationship and connection we provide. And as those humble people lower themselves in our presence, they reflect internally on what value they can provide us, leading us into a give-and-take relationship where everyone ends up satisfied.

Compare this line of thinking with the most narcissistic person you know. If and only if you are able to get into a conversation with a narcissist, that person constantly makes the conversation about him or herself. If you have a problem, he's had a worse one. If you are celebrating a success, she will one-up you. Such people are easily recognized because they seem like they are in a constant search for affirmation from others to overcompensate for an unrecognized lack of self-esteem. On the other hand, our humble companions exhibit what is often called a *quiet confidence*, meaning that, through mindful self-reflection, they understand their strengths and limitations, as well as where they stand with us, and as a result, such people seek to help others altruistically, rather than to tear them down to make themselves feel more powerful.

According to a 2014 study published in the journal, *Social Psychological and Personality Science*, gratitude and humility are intricately linked. The authors first defined humility as being marked by lower focus on the self, being more secure with oneself, and being able to recognize the value others present. They also noted that people with better humility tended to act with significantly less aggression, avoided manipulation of others, were far more honest, and also conserved resources more. In the end of their rigorous study, the authors were able to overwhelmingly conclude that gratitude and humility mutually reinforce one another. Therefore, by engaging in a regular gratitude practice (like the one you are still filling the margins of this book with), you are also increasing your humility quotient, which also makes you more likely to induce all the warm and fuzzy feelings in others that we described earlier while discussing how being around those with humility made us feel.

Humility as a Way to Lower Defenses

As a professional arguer and frequent instigator on social media, I have found myself in far more than my fair share of late-night flame wars. However, regardless of the person with whom I am arguing, I find that by treating that person with even the slightest dose of humility opens up doors to agreement that would otherwise be impossible. In fact, from what I have learned regarding the application of humility, I now teach many of my students who are involved in potentially controversial and/or divisive conversations online to utilize a patterned form of discussion response to invoke the spirit of humility. I explain the process as follows:

> *If you ever find yourself wanting to respond to someone's post because you feel a point must be argued or defended, there is a procedure you must follow. First, look for areas of common ground between your opinion and the other. Identify and explain those similarities before you move on to discussing points of disagreement. By doing this, we will maintain an atmosphere of mutual respect, where we value one another's views instead of shutting them down.*

In doing so, I have seen remarkably complex discussion between people of varying and seemingly opposite viewpoints arrive at the middle ground of compromise. By simply doing two things—acknowledging that we heard the other person's point of view and assigning value to some portion of that viewpoint—we use humility to open the door to greater understanding. This is especially easy to understand when we consider the opposite way of arguing, what with each party to the argument shouting increasingly louder, calling one another names, and basically resorting to nothing more than the use of ad hominem attacks on one another. In such situations, nobody learns anything, and each party walks away from the argument not having changed or altered their views a bit. However, by injecting merely a small measure of humility into the way one responds, emotion is kept in check and a bridge to understanding remains passable.

There is an interesting link between pride, appreciation, humility, and the expression of gratitude. We already know by this point in the book that expressing gratitude carries with it an amazing restorative power for our relationships. In this chapter, after your activity, you should take a moment to reflect on what it means to lower our defenses, set aside pride, and express appreciation for another person without any expectation of something in return. What does this do in most cases? What did it do in yours? What can we learn from this for our future?

Finally, to conclude this chapter, I have a short question for you before you move on, although it is potentially difficult to answer: Why does the expression of gratitude lower our defenses and open up lines of communication, even in the bleakest situations?

We will explore this and more in the next chapter, as we turn our attention to a leadership theory that presents us with a roadmap toward improving our orientation toward acting with greater humility.

CHAPTER 14

In the Service of Others

The servant-leader is servant first. It begins with the natural feeling that one wants to serve. Then, conscious choice brings one to aspire to lead. The best test is: do those served grow as persons; do they, while being served, become healthier, wiser, freer, more autonomous, more likely themselves to become servants? And, what is the effect on the least privileged in society; will they benefit, or, at least, not be further deprived?

—Robert Greenleaf

As I introduce a leadership theory as a way to explore humility and using service as a way of connecting more deeply with those whom we care about, it may seem a bit eccentric, even for someone as eccentric as myself. However, the concept of servant-leadership is actually the perfect place to start because it provides us with a roadmap toward developing greater interpersonal skills, as well as how to become an interpersonal leader. Of course, I'm not referring to leader as in the person in charge, barking orders and whatnot, but rather, the person who provides guidance and acts as a role model for others in interpersonal relationships, for such is the essence of interpersonal leadership.

While elements of the philosophy have been around since ancient times, such as passages from the Tao Te Ching, the Talmud, the Quran, and the Christian Bible, but the first person to coin the modern term of "servant-leadership" was a retired executive by the name of Robert Greenleaf in a 1970 essay, *The Servant as Leader*. The fundamental concept in Greenleaf's new approach to leadership is outlined in the quote that commences this chapter: "The servant-leader is servant first." Of course, this may sound remarkably familiar, as it closely connects to the chapter we just finished, as this leadership is fundamentally based on the concept of humility and the service of others. Greenleaf was essentially tired of leaders who commanded others, controlled others, and used their power for extensive personal gain, regardless of who it harmed in the process. Conversely, servant-leadership seeks to heal the damage caused by such leadership and instead look after the welfare of those being led by ensuring their well-being and potential for longer-term growth. Servant-leaders share power with those whom are led and place the needs of the many above their own needs. Examples of servant-leaders throughout history include Dr. Martin Luther King, Jr., Mahatma Gandhi, Nelson Mandela, Mother Teresa, and Eleanor Roosevelt, among many others. Servant-leaders often achieve greatness because of what they inspire in others, and in a chapter devoted to focusing on using service as a way to connect with others, this philosophy is a fantastic place to begin.

If you are wondering why the hyphen is used between the two words, it is intentional, as it has always been used to show the paradox or tension between the two terms, speaking to the balance sought between service and leading others.

To expand on Greenleaf's original work, former executive Larry Spears took up the servant-leadership charge and derived a set of ten characteristics of servant-leadership out of the original writings of Greenleaf. These characteristics do not stand alone, and they are not some form of checklist leading to an outcome. Each of the characteristics builds upon the last, and as one goes through the list, the concepts become more complex and difficult to put into practice. Those ten characteristics will become the basis for our adaption of the philosophy of servant-leadership to mindful interpersonal communication. Those ten characteristics include (in order): listening, empathy, healing, awareness, persuasion, conceptualization, foresight, stewardship, commitment to the growth of people, and building community.

Listening

As servant-leadership is a philosophy devoted to the well-being of others, it seems only appropriate to commence the ten characteristics with the more important half of communication. Listening is the foundation for the other ten characteristics because it is the fundamental method we can use to demonstrate a sincere commitment to others. Listening cannot be solely limited to that which we hear, but rather, we also listen using our eyes, with respect to nonverbal behaviors. Listening is a full-body activity that involves observation, but also reflection on what has been observed, what it all means, and how such observations can help with respect to serving others effectively. Servant-leaders are devoted listeners who practice the art of listening regularly and employ the correct listening style for the right context (see chapter 7 for a review of listening styles). Without a foundation in mindful listening, the other characteristics cannot blossom or develop.

Empathy

Servant-leadership, using the art of listening, employs empathy as a means to understand others fully, accepting and embracing others for the uniqueness and individual value. In using empathy, a servant-leader always assumes the best intentions when thinking of others' motivations, and even more importantly, the servant-leader does not completely reject others as potentially valuable people simply for mistakes in either the way they act or perform. When I think of the quality of empathy in leadership, I always think back to a story told to me by one of my leadership professors, who taught part-time so that he could serve his beloved alma mater and also happened to be the successful, self-made CEO of a pharmaceutical company. He told me of a time when a junior executive made a poor choice that ended up costing his company over a million dollars. As he realized the gravity of his mistake, he began cleaning out his office, and just as he did, the

CEO of the company walked in and asked what he was doing. "I'm cleaning out my desk, sir. I assumed I would be let go." The CEO laughed and replied, "Why would I let you go? I just spent a million dollars on training for you!" Such a situation requires looking at situations with an empathic, compassionate heart and being able to see the human side of such scenarios. Empathy requires the ability to listen carefully and mindfully with an open mind and the ability to discern various aspects of a situation.

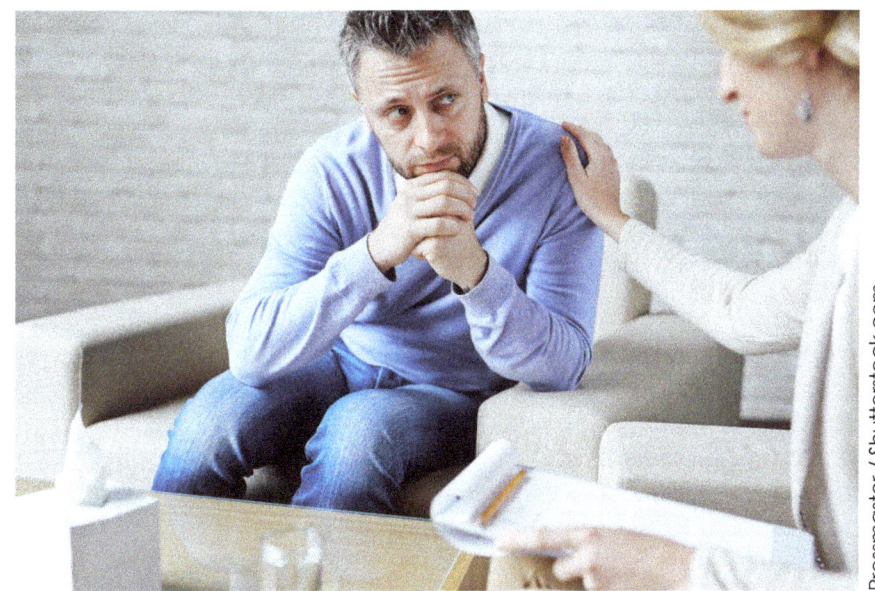

Healing

As listening takes place, and empathy develops as a result, the next characteristic begins to blossom, that of healing. Servant-leadership is different, in that it seeks not to destroy everything in its way, but rather, to provide healing for both the self and others. Servant-leadership, through its mindful use of empathy, recognizes that all people are essentially broken in some way and experience suffering from a diverse myriad of emotional states. Such brokenness is an essential part of the human condition, and servant-leaders recognize their duty and obligation to bring wholeness back to the human condition through the art of healing. In his seminal essay from 1970, Greenleaf wrote: "There is something subtle communicated to one who is being served and led if implicit in the compact between servant-leader and led is the understanding that the search for wholeness is something they share."

In her book, *Kitchen Table Wisdom*, Dr. Rachel Naomi Remen discussed the powerful story of a young man who had been seriously injured in an accident, effectively ending his athletic career. To help him cope with his loss, she had him do various forms of therapeutic drawing, at which point he drew a vase, and then took a black crayon, angrily scribbling all over the paper, stating that the scribbles represented the many cracks in the vase, all of which ruined it. Later in their sessions, Dr. Remen set the young man up with someone equally (if not more so) broken than he as a result of her own accident, and in the process of trying to help this young woman cope with her ordeal in the same was as he, the young man managed to work through his own emotional issues by way of serving hers. After successfully growing close to the young woman and eventually starting a relationship with her, the young man returned and asked Dr. Remen if he could have the drawing back. He then took a yellow crayon and began drawing one bold, bright line after another emanating out of the previously scribbled cracks in the vase. When asked about the yellow lines, the young man explained that we are all broken, but the cracks are what allow our light to shine outward for the sake of healing others.

Awareness

Where listening provides forensic evidence through mindful evidence gathering, empathy allows us to feel what others feel, and healing affords us the opportunity to serve others in an emotional capacity, awareness provides strength to servant-leaders by allowing them to increase their understanding of how issues affect themselves, others, and entire systems of interconnected components, leading to a greater and more holistic view of how such components affect and react with one another. As Greenleaf stated in his 1970 essay, "Awareness is not a giver of solace—it is just the opposite. It is a disturber and an awakener. Able leaders are usually sharply awake and reasonably disturbed. They are not seekers after solace. They have their own inner serenity." Ultimately, awareness is the capability of a person to look inward at her or his emotions and behavior, all the while considering how they intersect with our interpersonal relationships.

Persuasion

One of the greatest hallmarks of servant-leaders is their ability to bypass typical command-and-control approaches to leadership ("do as I say" leadership) and instead, take the considerably more difficult route of effectively persuading others. This approach tends to build commitment of followers, rather than merely obtaining compliance, which also breeds loyalty and respect, for followers who have been persuaded are not merely following orders, but they logically understand how their role contributes to the organization or to the relationship in which they have been persuaded. Persuasion builds off of the previous qualities because servant-leaders must listen mindfully to get to know others first, then use empathy to understand them fully, heal

wherever necessary before moving forward, all the while building an awareness of the intricate and interconnected nature of problems or issues affecting them and those being led. Only then can effective persuasion take place, because by that point, servant-leaders understand what information matters most to followers, and they use that information ethically to gain their loyalty and commitment. This process also tends to build consensus within groups, in addition to interpersonal relationships.

Conceptualization

Greenleaf often spoken of servant-leaders as the dreamers of great dreams. Managers often act as firefighters, moving from one problem to the next, all the while operating in reactionary modes and rarely think beyond their day-to-day reality. Servant-leaders, on the other hand, are able to see the "big picture" by looking beyond the obvious to see how various elements of their realities add up to contribute toward their longer-term goals. In an 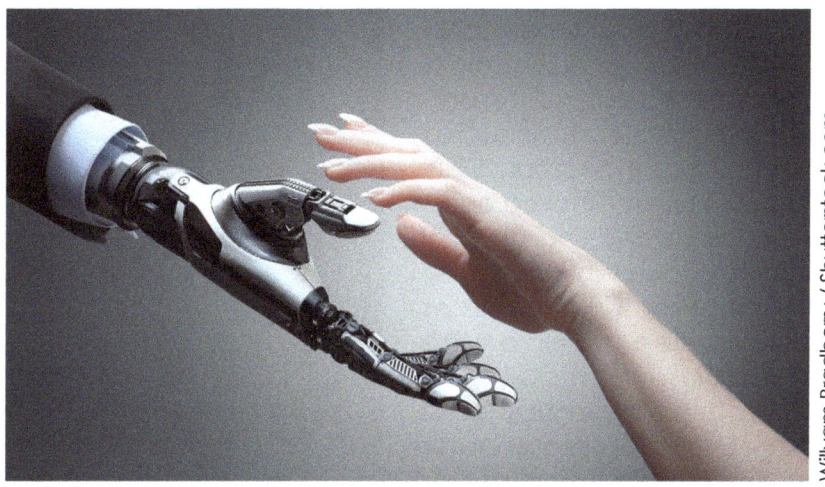 interpersonal relationship, this involves being able to see the very best qualities in our loved ones and understand how those qualities potentially add up to something larger that they may not necessarily be able to see for themselves, maybe because they are too focused on the minute details of day-to-day reality. Servant-leaders are able to provide overall vision and set greater goals, because they are able to conceptualize how all the little pieces go together, similar to using the completed picture of a puzzle to determine where to begin or what pieces need to go in which portion of the puzzle.

Foresight

The gift of foresight is one that requires success in the characteristic of conceptualization. A potential servant-leader must be able to see the bigger picture before foresight can take place, but when it does, such a person is able to connect the dots, so to speak, between the lessons of the past, the reality of the present moment, and the most possible outcome resulting from their decisions leading toward the future. Think of foresight as being related heavily to intuition and gut feelings, but when applied, becomes more of an art form than a misunderstood alternative to psychic predictions.

Stewardship

Stewardship is the act of mindfully caring for something on behalf of another through the process of trust. As a leader, there is a responsibility to care for the wide diversity of resources at stake in an organization or within interpersonal relationships. For example, a leader in an organization has a responsibility to be a steward of financial resources, material goods, and human resources. Interpersonal relationships, at first glance, may seem vastly different, but a servant-leader in such a context has the responsibility to look after their loved ones' emotional well-being, physical health, and possibly even their financial/material resources as well, depending on the situation. To be a steward is to practice the principles of accountability (see chapter 8). Servant-leadership beings with the presumption that such a person looks after the welfare and needs of others in their care first and foremost, and to accomplish this, such leaders are honest, transparent, and use persuasion rather than outright control.

Commitment to the Growth of People

Whereas leadership in other, more traditional forms, such as command-and-control leadership, are often focused primarily on development and growth of the individual above all others, servant-leadership seeks first to develop others instead. Servant-leaders are able to recognize that, by investing in the growth and development of those in their care and stewardship, they effectively also grow and develop their organization as a whole, which in turn, is for the greater good of the group. By growing and developing as a group, the organization becomes significantly stronger, and in turn, so does the leader. Maintaining such a commitment often requires the earlier characteristics of

conceptualization and foresight to develop the ability to recognize growth potential and where such investments need to be made. Servant-leaders genuinely believe that the people in their care possess intrinsic value and not merely their more obvious contributions as members of the group or organization.

Building Community

Servant-leaders recognize that, all too often in the Age of Distraction, humans are losing their sense of community as we gravitate toward virtual interactions with hundreds or even thousands of people at a time, effectively being swallowed up or absorbed into groups too large to feel our humanity. This use of the characteristic of awareness, combined with the commitment to the growth of people, causes servant-leaders to seek out means to develop more of a sense of community on behalf of those within their stewardship. Greenleaf, in his 1970 essay, stated:

> *All that is needed to rebuild community as a viable life form for large numbers of people is for enough servant-leaders to show the way, not by mass movements, but by each servant-leader demonstrating his own unlimited liability for a quite specific community-related group.*

For example, a business leader devoted to the pursuit of servant-leadership might seek out ways to make the organization feel more like a family and less like a stereotypical profit-driven business. Servant-leaders as parents might seek to deepen family connections and increase quality time spent together as a family unit. Educators employing servant-leadership spend considerable time developing and practicing methods to enhance their connections with students to become more meaningful, memorable, and open. Often, such methods, regardless of context, will employ several of the other ten characteristics of servant-leadership in conjunction with one another to achieve this sense of community over time.

Tying All the Characteristics Together

While the previous ten items are incredibly powerful and present amazing possibilities to deepen and develop relationships in just about any context, from work to family or from friends to romantic partners, they are not intended to be an exhaustive list of the requirements for servant-leadership. Larry Spears, the author who developed this list from Greenleaf's writings, once said that they simply serve to communicate the power and potential that the theory of servant-leadership offers to those who are up to taking on the challenge. However, one of the biggest problems with servant-leadership today is that far too many people read up on it, become inspired, and think that they can become servant-leaders just by reading a book, attending a class, or simply making the decision to suddenly become a servant-leader. On the contrary, developing servant-leadership, as you might imagine, requires a steady, long-term commitment to the development of each of these characteristics.

In fact, think of each characteristic as a new language. Learning to listen, for example, is a skill that takes considerable time and practice, and in learning and perfecting this elusive skill, it effectively changes one's personal sense of culture in much the same manner that learning a language may develop. Committing to servant-leadership is the type of endeavor that could potentially take years to refine and cultivate through a rigorous process of painful experience, as well as trial and error. As a result of this realization, our next activity is to develop a simple strategy regarding how we might utilize just one or more of the characteristics right now in our pursuit of the one issue or problem you've chosen to pursue during your journey through this book (such as the one picked in chapter 8 and refined in chapter 12).

Activity: Those Who Want to Rule Must First Learn to Serve

For the sake of context, the symbol pictured on the right comes from Ghana, in western Africa, from the Asante tribe, and it is one symbol from among many that can be found on cloth, walls, and pottery, all called Adinkra symbols. This one is called "Nea ope se obedi hene," and the English translation is, "He who wants to be king must first learn to serve." I have always found this to be a powerful concept (so personal and powerful to me that I had it tattooed), and this is our opportunity to explore it further.

Knowing what we now know about the 10 characteristics of servant-leadership, I want you to draft up a plan to commence the practice servant-leadership in some aspect of your life related to your chosen issue from chapters 8 and 12, whether at work, at home, in your community, or at school. Make it a short-term plan with a realistic goal in mind, based off of one or more of the ten characteristics of a servant-leader.

I have been using the example of social media addiction, so in this case, I might select the characteristics of listening, empathy, awareness, and healing to address the impact of social media addiction in my home life. I would then write up a short-term plan as follows:

- **Listening.** I will sit down with my wife and children at separate times and ask them how my abuse of social media makes them feel. During this interaction, I commit to listening mindfully, avoid defending myself at all costs, and will take notes for subsequent steps of this plan.
- **Empathy.** As I learn more about the impact of my social media addiction, I will empathize with my family by using my imagination to determine how I would feel if I were in their position, thereby validating their feelings and affording me the opportunity to empathize.
- **Awareness.** I will keep a 48-hour log of all the times I either actively participate in social media or simply check for notifications. I anticipate that this log will be rather eye-opening, as it will make me more aware of just how much time I truly waste on this addiction.
- **Healing.** Once I understand the impact my abuse of social media has on those in my family and I am more aware of the extent of my use and abuse, I will seek healing by devising a plan to cut down or even eliminate the use of social media from my home life, and I will do so in conjunction with my family's input and advice.

Notes

Post-Activity Reflection

If we look at the greatest leaders in history, we can easily notice a pretty common thread. Most of them employed humility to accurately self-assess their weaknesses and surround themselves with people who supplemented those weaknesses. In interpersonal and organizational relationships, however, we often find the exact opposite case occurring. We more often gravitate to those we like and those who make us feel comfortable. Unfortunately, conflict is rarely comfortable, so as a result, many of us choose to avoid it, which is one of the reasons why we are working through this book.

For this chapter's conclusion, reflect on how you now feel about approaching conflict as a servant-leader, having explored so many new methods and tools for looking at it differently, using a lens of compassion and other-centeredness. Do you now feel a bit more confident about letting go of pride and approaching conflict with humility and a sincere interest to serve, as well as healing the relationship? Why or why not?

CHAPTER 15

Question Everything

He who asks a question is a fool for five minutes.

He who never asks a question remains a fool for a lifetime.

—Chinese Proverb

In 1980, a young doctoral student called David Cooperrider began laying the groundwork for a fundamental shift in thinking, which he would later name, *appreciative inquiry* (AI). To illustrate exactly what AI is and how it drastically changes the way we look at self-improvement, as well as organizational problem solving, let's take a look at a hypothetical situation based on a true organizational success story...

Imagine a manufacturing company, Company X, that makes widgets (an imaginary product), and let's imagine that Company X has earned a staggering 90% customer satisfaction rate, meaning that, after purchasing one of their widgets, 9 out of 10 of their customers end up somewhere along a spectrum of product satisfaction, ranging from "this product is pretty cool" to "this product absolutely changed my life." Those are actually pretty great numbers to an outside viewer, but within many modern organizations, leaders at the top of the proverbial food chain might likely look at such results and ask, "How can we improve?" To do so, that Company X would likely examine the remaining 10% of customers who fell on the spectrum of dissatisfaction, ranging from "I was unimpressed" to "I will never do business with you again, and I will warn others to stay away from you as well." After exploring these results, Company X might hire a consultant to assist them would likely examine the 10% of dissatisfied customers and then put a task force together that analyzes their manufacturing processes to identify where problems are occurring, who is responsible for defects, and how they can fix those problems. So far, so good, right? Sound like a typical organization? You may have experienced similar situations before, even if not at work. Think of being a kid whose math grade just dropped from an A to a C. Your parents may have likely said, "What went wrong, and how are you going to fix this?" What these scenarios represent are our typically assumed and ingrained approach to problems, to conflicts, and to life in general most of the time.

Cooperrider's approach effectively flips these scenarios on their proverbial heads. In the real-life story, Company X had the foresight to hire an appreciative inquiry (AI) consultant to work with them on their 10% problem. However, that consultant walked in on the first day and said, "Wow, your company has a 90% satisfaction rate? That's incredible!" The consultant then set up an analysis team that examined the spectrum of satisfied customers, rather than those who were dissatisfied, with a special focus on those who were at the far end of the spectrum and said the product was absolutely life-changing. That analysis determined what the variables were that led to that level of success, rather than trying to figure out what was causing the problems. The analysis included interviews and observations of the employees who were responsible for making the product so well, from manufacturing to shipping, in addition to examining the various sales relationships nurtured along the way with those particularly thrilled customers.

Simply put, AI is an approach that, instead of being problem-focused, is strengths-based. AI seeks to discover what strengths lead to success and then develops strategies to incorporate those strengths into various processes. In other words, build upon past success using existing strengths and problems will likely dissipate on their own. AI, however, is not without its critics, and you may have even thought of a painfully obvious critique as you read the previous paragraph. First, AI is not Pollyannaish, it is not a philosophy blinded by looking through rose-colored lenses, nor is it blindly optimistic. Simply put, if AI does not ignore problems in the hopes that they will go away, then how does it work to reduce problems at all?

pathdoc / Shutterstock.com

We humans are naturally hardwired to seek out negativity. This is a skill that was born out of necessity back when our highest three priorities as animals were finding sustenance, not being killed, and reproducing. In those times, day-to-day survival dictated that we constantly assess our surroundings for potential dangers and hazards, and such behavior became ingrained within our very DNA as our animal instinct. Therefore, it is no surprise that, today, we continue to mindlessly and automatically seek out negativity as a way of assessing threats and hazards, even if those threats are nothing more than gossip about our favorite celebrities or the grocery store being completely out of cookie dough ice cream (we all have our priorities—don't judge me). If this isn't a compelling enough explanation, then take a look for yourself at any magazine in the grocery store checkout line (ideally while holding a pint of cookie dough ice cream as you read through them) or peruse your social media feed. There is literally negativity just about everywhere you look, and people feed off of it. Even mass media and news organizations have a tendency to gravitate toward the negative with guiding philosophies such as, "If it bleeds, it leads." If you turn on the news or peruse a typical news website or social media page, this becomes painfully evident. If you're lucky, you might find a positively oriented story buried lower on the page or presented as a human interest piece at the tail end of a newscast.

What AI provides is a fundamental shift in the tendency to focus on the negative by radically and consciously shifting mindset and focus. It proposes that we set aside the negative and instead, examine our past successes to determine what made them successful as a method of learning from our wins rather than our mistakes. As we apply our strengths to various situations, then those strengths have the tendency to overcome problems in creative, innovative ways, and as a result, the problems fade into the background.

Remember Company X? Of course you do, since it was only three paragraphs ago. Company X really did exist, and within about a six-month period, using AI as their guiding philosophy, they effortlessly raised their satisfaction rate by another whopping 8%, to an astonishing overall satisfaction rate of 98%. Of the 2% remaining, they managed to narrow the spectrum of dissatisfied to range from "this product just wasn't right for me" to "I think I ordered the wrong product." Even among their dissatisfied 2% of customers, they managed to reduce the level of dissatisfaction to a more reasonable level, effectively eliminating disgruntled former customers. Additionally, as an unexpected side bonus, all employees within the organization, from front line assembly workers to upper level sales associates, began exhibiting greater work satisfaction, less turnover, greater retention, and the organization began seeing higher cost savings, as employees began feeling more invested in the organization and thus, sought new and innovative ways to conserve company resources.

If this all sounds too good to be true, and you're still skeptical, then let's try a quick little exercise to demonstrate the immense and immediate power of AI. For this activity, we first need to understand how AI-type questions are composed successfully. AI utilizes what are called *powerful questions* to dig at the root of where strengths may lie. A powerful question is thought-provoking, expands upon possibilities, generates curiosity, challenges assumptions, and provides focus. Composing a powerful question begins with knowing how to construct such an inquiry. A yes/no question is not considered a powerful question because it fails to achieve the above goals. Who/when/where/what questions are only slightly more effective because, even though they are open-ended, they still elicit highly specific responses. The *most* powerful questions begin with what/how/why, and what-if. To illustrate, take a look at the following progression of question editing, from least to most powerful:

- Are you passing math right now?
- What parts are you struggling with the most in math right now?
- How might you raise your grade in math?
- Why do you think your current topics in math are so challenging?
- What if you could use what you already know about math and apply it, along with a peer tutor, to what you are studying right now?

Notice the change in tone and feel to those questions? What began as more of an interrogation ends on a compassionate and inclusive note that puts the person at ease and stimulates more reflection and thought.

In addition to structure, we also need to examine the questions for implicit assumptions. In the example questions above, there are clear assumptions arising out of the questions:

- Are you passing math right now?
  - Assumption: *You are probably not passing math.*
- What parts are you struggling with the most in math right now?
  - Assumption: *You are currently struggling with math.*
- How might you raise your grade in math?
  - Assumption: *You have the ability to raise your grade in math.*
- Why do you think your current topics in math are so challenging?
  - Assumption: *Parts of math can be challenging for anyone.*
- What if you could use what you already know about math and apply it, along with a peer tutor, to what you are studying right now?
  - Assumption: *You already possess inherent strengths that can be paired with outside assistance to better understand math.*

Again, note the change in feel and tone in these assumptions as they slowly shift from blame and a problem-focused approach toward a compassionate, positive, and strengths-based approach. Appreciative inquiry forces not only the questioner but also those being questioned to flip their ways of thinking to look at a situation, issue, problem, or scenario from a strength-based perspective.

Activity: Appreciative Inquiry Interview

It is now your turn to experience the potential power of even the simplest AI interview. Compose four AI questions using the information on how to create powerful questions above, and interview a friend or loved one. Pay close attention to not only the content of the responses to your questions, but also to the general tone and feel of your interaction. Observe vocal tone, volume, posture, gestures, and use of time during the interview. Try to determine how this interaction differs from your typical everyday interactions with this person.

For your convenience, as well as to spark creativity, here are some AI questions you may either use verbatim or, at the very least, build from to compose your questions:

- Tell me the story of what you consider to be your greatest success and the conditions that helped you achieve that success.
- Within your daily life, what elements would you say revitalize you the most and make you feel most alive?
- What fun activity from your childhood do you wish you could revive, and how do you think incorporating that activity would impact your daily routine?
- What if you could wake up tomorrow and suddenly be wildly successful at just one aspect of your life? What would that be and why?

Write down your questions below, leaving a few lines between each one. Then, during the interview, take notes on the interaction that follows each one, including the way the person responded to the question—not the answers to the questions themselves, but rather, the nonverbal tone that accompanied those responses, including the amount of time and subsequent conversation that went along with those responses. Feel free to engage in follow-up questions and further discussion surrounding the question, including your responses to the same question if the moment calls for it. Allow discussion following your questions to be fluid and organic, and avoid providing too much structure, save for the original questions.

Question 1:
___
___
___
___
___
___

Question 2:

Question 3:

Question 4:

Dissecting the AI Interview Process

Appreciative inquiry is a method of discovering the best in people and one that finds what works rather than what's wrong, thereby capitalizing on those strengths for the future. For example, a powerful, successful weightlifter will not dwell on the 10 times she was unable to deadlift a personal record attempt and why she could not successfully lift the weight. Instead, she will focus on what she did *right* to break her last record and continue to experiment with new means of doing the same by perfecting her form and capitalizing on her strengths and abilities while still refining technique. Yet, in most organizations and relationships, including families, we have a tendency to look solely at what is wrong and how we can fix it.

If your four-question interview was anything like the hundreds of my students who have gone before you with this activity, then you likely experienced the following:

- More pronounced, animated gestures
- Smiles with greater frequency and authenticity
- Sustained laughter
- Lengthy, well-articulated responses
- Connections between personal experience and the power of those moments
- Losing track of time, leading to significantly deeper conversations
- Sparks of raw creativity, little things that remind you each of stories worthy of sharing for the sake of connecting on certain points
- Meandering away from the original points, tangential discussion
- A general feeling of connection with one another as you share your thoughts on the qualities that make life worth living

The late basketball coach and sports commentator, Jim Valvano (Jimmy V), once noted that, to live a full life, there are three things we should do each day. We should spend some time in thought, we should laugh, and we should allow our emotions to move us to tears. Conversations such as this AI interview often check off all three of these requirements, which begs the question, why don't we interact like this more often? Essentially, AI rewires the brain by forcing us to flip questions we assume as being normal, which leads us into another method specifically designated for flipping questions.

Positive Deviance

Recently, I was introduced to a system that is closely related to appreciative inquiry, yet remains another approach to question-flipping called *positive deviance* (PD). If you're anything like me, when you see the word, deviance, your interest is immediately piqued. According to the Positive Deviance Initiative (positivedeviance.org), the system is defined as follows:

> *Positive deviance is based on the observation that, in every community, there are certain individuals or groups whose uncommon behaviors and strategies enable them*

to find better solutions to problems than their peers, while having access to the same resources and facing similar or worse challenges.

Essentially, PD goes into seemingly impossible situations, searches for people who defy all odds and succeed somehow, and examines what makes such success possible. As a result, PD often uncovers seemingly "hidden" resources that often cost absolutely nothing more than flipping the question. To illustrate, allow me to share a few enlightening stories that I first heard from a leading expert on positive deviance, Dr. Arvind Singhal, as they help us make the essence of PD clear.

Nasreddin Hodja

In many parts of Central Asia (primarily Turkey), stories are told about a Sufi called Nasreddin Hodja, often remembered for his wise lessons hidden among humorous anecdotes. In this particular story, Nasreddin announced to his entire village that he was taking up a career as an "honest smuggler" and bravely dared everyone to catch him, seemingly bragging about his skill as a smuggler.

Soon after, Nasreddin was walking toward the border at the edge of his country. He led eight donkeys by a rope, and each donkey was laden with straw and bags. A customs officer, who had heard Nasreddin's dare earlier, saw Nasreddin coming, and he smiled, rubbing his hands together with glee. "Ah, here comes the 'great' Nasreddin, and he must be trying to smuggle something past me." Turning to his fellow border officials, he mumbled, "Watch this. I will find the smuggled goods, and surely take Nasreddin up on his dare."

The customs officer stopped Nasreddin, saying, "Greetings, oh great Nasreddin! Before you can cross, you must allow me to search your donkeys, because I suspect you are attempting to smuggle goods across the border."

Nasreddin nodded in approval. "Be my guest, good sir, but I'm afraid you will not find what you think you are looking for."

The customs officer scowled at Nasreddin, responding, "Everyone knows you're a smuggler. You announced it to the entire village."

Nasreddin nodded again, and the customs officer began searching the donkeys meticulously. He dismantled bundles of straw, opened the bags strapped to them all, and even called to the other officers to assist and provide another set of eyes. However, as hard as the customs officials tried, they found nothing hidden among Nasreddin's caravan, so they had no choice but to send him on his way across the border.

A week later, Nasreddin returned to the border crossing, once again leading eight donkeys laden with straw and other packages. "Ah, Nasreddin, we meet again," the customs officer said to him, "I bet you think we won't search you as closely as last time, but you are dead wrong." The officer called to all available customs official, and a dozen men picked through everything in sight, making quite the mess as they went along. But once again, they found nothing at all and had no choice but to let Nasreddin pass.

The next week, the same event occurred and every week for many months. Nasreddin led his donkeys to the border, and every time, the customs officer glared at Nasreddin with the greatest suspicion. As time passed, the officer's determination to expose Nasreddin as a smuggler grew more and more determined, and each week, his searches took longer and became more methodical, but each week, the officer found nothing of value.

Nasreddin never lost his temper, and he never became upset with the searches. He would stand and wait patiently while the searches were conducted, and he even began to bring refreshments to sit back and relax while the customs officer grew increasingly disappointed.

Years passed, and word of the searches spread far and wide. Neighboring townspeople wondered what Nasreddin could be smuggling and how he got the items past the customs inspections. Were they coins, gold, or gemstones? As a result of the rumors, Nasreddin's reputation as an ingenious smuggler spread to every town and across every nearby border.

Persistently, the customs officer was bound and determined to undo Nasreddin, and his determination grew more with each time he witnessed Nasreddin's peaceful demeanor. This cat-and-mouse game continued for years and then decades. The customs officer grew old and soon became old enough to retire, but he said, "I cannot stop working until I have discovered Nasreddin's secret." So, he continued to work, well past retirement age and deep into a ripe, old age. However, the time came when he was simply far too tired to work. His back ached, his eyes were failing him, and he could barely stand any longer, so he finally, at long last, retired from his post. However, he never stopped thinking of Nasreddin, his nemesis. How did he do it, the customs officer continued wondering? Perhaps, he thought, they should have slaughtered one of the donkeys to see if maybe Nasreddin had forced them to swallow precious gems and gold.

But, shortly after the customs officer retired, Nasreddin joined him in retirement and stopped crossing the border. The two men eventually turned their adversarial relationship into friendship. One day, the officer and Nasreddin were enjoying coffee together and reminiscing about old times, when the officer bluntly said, "Nasreddin, I cannot rest any longer. I know, without a doubt, that all those years were spent smuggling something, am I right?"

Nasreddin smiled that same familiar, patient smile, and slowly, he nodded.

"Please, Nasreddin," the officer pleaded, "You must tell me. Was it gold? Silver? Gemstones? Where did you hide them?"

With each successive guess by the officer, Nasreddin continued smiling his patient smile and shook his head.

"Nasreddin, I will never be able to rest until I know. Please, now that we have both retired and are too old to do anything about it, tell me. Give me the truth so that an old man can rest!"

Nasreddin smile again, leaned forward, and whispered to the officer, "Okay, I will tell you now. All those years, I was smuggling donkeys."

Flipped Questions

Abraham Lincoln was, as of this writing, the tallest president in United States history, standing at nearly 6'4". A popular battlefield story of Lincoln recounts that, as a soldier approached Lincoln, he saluted and then extended his hand for a handshake, of course thrusting it upward toward the towering president. At that point, the soldier

remarked, "Wow, you are tall! How tall are you?" Lincoln replied, "Like you, son, tall enough so that my feet reach the ground."

Mother Teresa once, on a visit to New York to speak at the United Nations General Assembly, was walking through the city when she was approached by a group of people who wanted to meet and speak with her. Always being one to engage people in conversation, Mother Teresa obliged. The people identified themselves as being with an organized group of protestors who were planning an antiwar demonstration in protest of U.S. involvement in Vietnam, and they asked Mother Teresa if she would honor their efforts by attending and possibly speaking at their rally. Much to their surprise, Mother Teresa shook her head no and explained to the protestors that she could not possibly participate in an antiwar demonstration. Shocked, the protestors asked why, to which she responded, "I will never attend an antiwar rally, but as soon as you have a pro-peace rally, I'll be there."

Mahatma Gandhi, perhaps one of the best-known figures of the late-19th and early 20th centuries, famous for his philosophy of nonviolence and civil disobedience, was revered as the father of modern India, having been an instrumental figure in obtaining India's independence from Britain. However, as Gandhi traveled around India, he always did so via the cheapest and simplest form of travel, usually third-class rail, much to the disappointment of his admirers. They would constantly ask, "Bapu (Father), why would you dishonor us by traveling third class? Why won't you let us honor you by putting you in first class accommodations?" To this question, he simply replied, "Because there is no fourth class."

Positive Deviance in Action

You may be wondering what Nasreddin, Abe Lincoln, Mother Teresa, and Gandhi all have in common with respect to these stories and what the common thread is that binds them together. In each story, we see examples of what it means to flip questions. In Nasreddin's story, the customs official was blinded by his own assumptions, that what he was looking for fit a very specific and narrow description, when the answer was in front of him the whole time. In Lincoln's story, rather than responding typically by telling the soldier his measured height, Lincoln placed himself on equal footing with the soldier (pun totally intended) by starting with, "Like you, son," and continuing to suggest that their height difference did not matter, seeing as how their feet both reached the ground. Mother Teresa challenged the protestors, who clearly had a goal of eliminating war, by implying the question, what are you truly for? Is it merely to end war, or is it to promote peace instead? Finally, Gandhi's story, his humility and dedication to living simply was legendary. As long as there existed inequality in India, Gandhi refused to take part in a class system that served to oppress the poor, and when asked the question, his simple response forced those asking the question to reconsider their views. All of this is the essence of positive deviance.

thi / Shutterstock.com

One of the most well-known and successful outcomes of the use of positive deviance comes out of Vietnam. A leading organization devoted to the application of positive deviance was tasked by government officials in Vietnam to address the issue of child malnutrition, and furthermore, they were told to show results in only six months. The organization immediately set to working with families in rural Vietnam, seeking first to discover families whose children seemed to be well nurtured, despite all the odds that poverty threw in their way. Such families were raising strong, healthy children, but were doing so without any added benefits or resources as compared to other families where the mortality rate was significantly higher. The team studied everything about these families' routines, as they presented cases of positive deviance. They were positive in the sense that whatever they were doing was working, and they were deviants because something about their routines challenged the status quo.

Early in the organization's study, they discovered that the families had been gathering abundant, yet tiny shrimps and crabs from rice fields, and they added those along with sweet potato greens to their children's meals. Most people (myself included) would not think of eating the greens, mainly because it's the sweet potato that I'm after for a Thanksgiving feast, but these families were resourceful and used all at their disposal, including the part of the plant that nobody else was eating, a part of the plant that turned out to be high in nutrients and antioxidants. Additionally, the families were feeding their children three to four times each day, rather than the two meals a day that were customary among other families.

Based upon these findings, the organization made recommendation to families with malnourished children to start gathering the tiny shrimps and crabs, as well as add sweet potato greens to their children's meals and increase the frequency of feeding. Within six months, several hundred malnourished children became healthy, and the program was then spread to other communities as well, resulting in a wide, sweeping change in the health of Vietnamese children everywhere. What these researchers did was to challenge assumptions (feeding twice/day, throwing out greens, etc.) in much the same way as Nasreddin did with his donkeys, Lincoln did with approach to height, Mother Teresa did with long-term goals, and Gandhi did with humility.

Applied to interpersonal interaction, positive deviance can challenge any and all of our assumptions of the way in which interpersonal interaction "should" take place. For example, some professors may choose to hold their office hours not in their offices, but off-campus, at a local coffee shop, where students can show up and engage in material further or seek advice away from the typical humdrum of campus life. Another example comes from the fact that, at my institution, I am horribly spoiled by having a beautiful beach only a quarter-mile from my classrooms, and as such, when weather permits, we will go hold our classes on the beach. Simply changing scenery for a discussion can be powerful enough to evoke creativity from all involved, leading to more mindful, present, and ultimately, memorable interactions.

Prison Guards in Denmark

To provide one last example of the application of positive deviance to interactions, let us explore a fascinating scenario from Denmark. Prison guards are notorious for having high turnover, especially among this one specific prison from Denmark. It seemed as though prison guards were operating through a revolving door system, and they simply could not keep guards for various reasons: burnout, prisoner abuse, guards being injured by prisoners, etc. So, an organization specializing in PD was brought in to examine the situation. Immediately, the organization set out to locate guards seemingly unaffected by the conditions that had caused other guards to leave in a hurry. Among the guards they found, they all seemed to have significantly higher job satisfaction, and all of these guards in the case study were well respected by the inmates of the prison. After sitting and discussing with each guard their rituals in an attempt to discover what works where nothing else seemed plausible, they discovered the following behaviors:

- One guard proudly talked about the tours he gave to new inmates. As new prisoners arrived, the guard would tour each one around the prison, showing them where everything could be found and explaining the "ropes" to them as a method of orientation.
- Another guard stated that he refused to read the inmates' files because he was afraid that, if he knew their crimes, he might treat them differently or poorly.
- A third guard described a bathroom ritual he performed with all inmates (inmates at this prison did not have plumbing in their cells, and cells were private, with solid doors and no bars to be

able to see people coming). Most guards, when asked to come relieve an inmate by taking him to the restroom, would grumble and complain, make the inmates wait a painful amount of time, or rough up the inmate getting in and out of their cells. This guard, however, jingled his keys as he approached, so that the inmate would know he was coming. Then, he would knock on the cell door, announcing that he was there to relieve the inmate. After taking the inmate to the restroom, he would open the door for the inmate, allow him to re-enter his cell, and then *ask* the inmate if he was ready for him to close the door before closing it gently and turning the lock slowly, so as to not make the dreaded clang, which, to a prisoner, is symbolic of hopelessness and being trapped. When pressed for an explanation, the guard simply stated that it was his way of providing a basic sense of human dignity to these men, despite their crimes.

As a result of these insights, the Danish prison system underwent sweeping reforms, which led to a radical decrease in recidivism, more effective resocialization, and a healthier working environment.

Activity: Positively Deviant Behavior

As with appreciative inquiry earlier, it is now time for use to experiment with positive deviance, and for this activity, you are going to pick a fight. Mindful presence is an act of defiance. For you to be fully present, you need to defy the very distractions tugging at your attention, which involves questioning your priorities at any given moment and deviating from assumed truths and principles. In picking this fight, you are asking three universal questions that mock conventional or regular ways of being:

- Why do I have to act this way?
- Why can't I do things differently?
- What is stopping me from doing it my way?

These impulses guide our creativity and moments of sheer, unadulterated presence. Ultimately, every act of creation is also an act of destruction or abandonment—disappearing into the moment and casting aside the rest to make way for the new.

So, I want you to pick a fight—not that kind of fight. Pick a fight with the system, the rules, your rituals, or even your everyday routines. For one day, be completely contrary, to the point of being ornery and belligerent with anything and everything you do. In essence, turn everything upside down. For example:

- Defy your normal alarm and wake up an hour or two early to take in the sunrise;
- Do your normal workout routine in reverse or twice as fast (or twice as slow);
- Leave early, and instead of your normal route, take a long, scenic route you normally don't have time for;
- Pick a fight with your usual impulses—question what's gone unquestioned in your brain for far too long;

These are private exercises. There's no need to pick fights with other people—you are only competing with yourself. It is fairly well known that many artists engage in this activity to generate their creative side. Beethoven was well known for starting wars with his compositions. He couldn't operate as an artist without the feeling that he was at war with someone or something. Placing ourselves into fighting mode forces change and liberates the creative mind.

Reflecting on our Newfound Deviant Behaviors

After having done both activities for this chapter, spend some time reflecting on each of the following, some of which employs AI, PD, or a mix of both. Consider answering the questions right here, in the book, using the margins and/or the space between each one, as you may wish to come back to your responses in the near future.

- When was the last time you remember experiencing an interaction like the one you experienced during your AI interview? If it was long ago, then why? Why not interact like this more frequently? What is stopping you, and what can you do to facilitate interaction like this more often?
- In what activities do you tend to experience a sense of "disappearance" (i.e., the rest of the world seems to fade away) most often? In other words, what do you do that causes you to temporarily forget all of life's issues and problems and absorb yourself into the moment, regardless of consequence? What is it about this activity that captivates you so? How can you utilize that knowledge to become more present in other walks of your life?
- Spend some time mulling over the mistakes you've made throughout your life, big, small, or anywhere in between. Then, examine them and ask yourself the AI question, what if you had things to do all over again, would you have done things differently, or has the inherent value in that mistake experience made it an integral part of who you are today?
- Now, think about your future mistakes. No, don't try to identify where you might screw up in the future, but rather, think about your *orientation* toward mistakes using a lens comprised of both appreciative inquiry and/or positive deviance. Mistakes *will* happen to us all, but how will you react next time you make a mistake, after having given this chapter some serious thought? What will it take for you to view a mistake as a challenge, an opportunity for learning, growth, and development, or as a moment of real value?

Conclusion

Drink your tea slowly and reverently, as if it is the axis on which the world earth revolves, slowly, evenly, without rushing toward the future; live the actual moment.

Only this moment is life.

—Thich Nhat Hanh

During our journey throughout this book, we have explored the concept of mindfulness from many diverse angles. We started by exploring its basic four components (awareness, intention, learning to notice novelty as it arises, and nonjudgmental acceptance of that which occurs in the moment). We then moved to learning about how mindful behaviors can help us through the bustle and stress of life amid the Age of Distraction. After some of the darkest portions of our journey, we turned back toward a lighter side as we examined the relation of mindfulness to qualities such as resilience, vulnerability, and gratitude, as well as how practicing mindfulness can lead us to a greater sense of appreciation as we notice more opportunities to savor some of the best moments life has to offer.

Throughout the material, we have tried our hands at many opportunities to put mindfulness into practice, some of which were considerably more difficult and/or uncomfortable than others. We began by promoting a greater sense of self-awareness, which of course, is difficult, because we don't always like what we learn about ourselves. Next, we attempted to become more comfortable being alone with our thoughts, the challenged the boundaries of our comfort zones in various ways, and finally, the pinnacle of discomfort came when we actually had to seek out some of the most potentially hurtful and critical feedback possible—on purpose! The only other activity within this book that competes for the title of most uncomfortable (though necessary) was the time when we sought forgiveness and learned how such an act can restore relationships and repair communication.

Fortunately, we were able to leave all that behind in the second half of the book, where we had the opportunities to experience what it's like to truly savor the moment, along with nurturing a spirit of gratitude (you are still writing down your five items at the start of your day, right?), but we lifted gratitude off the pages of this book and put our newfound appreciation to the test by learning about how expressing such gratitude can foster humility, deepen relationships, and effectively promote some of the best relational qualities we could ever hope to discover. Lastly, our activities brought us to this point, where we have now experimented with the concepts of servant-leadership, appreciative inquiry, and positive deviance, all of which can be employed in our everyday lives to radically transform the way we interact with others.

As you likely recall, we took the opportunity every fourth chapter to systematically explore how mindfulness and its associated characteristics can help us work through a specific issue or situation. We started back in chapter 4 by conducting a communication audit on ourselves to identify various shortcomings or opportunities for improvement with respect to our various communicative abilities, from nonverbal decoding to intercultural awareness, and from listening abilities to interpersonal empathy. The results of that audit provided the initial list from which we narrowed it down to one specific issue or situation we wanted to work on further. Later, we first examined at the conclusion of chapter 8 how that issue or situation might benefit by applying either qualities that contribute to resilience (learning to accept criticism, letting go of our egos, seeking forgiveness, listening, and embracing vulnerability). By chapter 12, we were looking at qualities that contribute to savoring (presence, letting go of distraction, and gratitude).

After 15 chapters, we have now reached the concluding chapter of our journey, and as such, we need to return to where we last looked at the issue or situation we have been working with. Since concluding Chapter 12, we have examined principles of humility by way of gratitude, servant-leadership, appreciative inquiry, and positive deviance. Unlike the concepts discussed prior to chapter 13, our most recent topics are more systematic and present us with the potential for longer-term, strategic, and lasting change. As such, we now need to apply these to our chosen topics in such a way as to devise a sustainable and ongoing strategy to address or resolve our chosen issue or situation.

To begin, return briefly to the activities and reflections you completed for chapters 4, 8, and 12, and analyze the information you compiled so far, looking for evidence of development in relation to the issue or situation you chose to address. Once you have not only re-familiarized yourself with your chosen issue, along with how far you've come by this point, I want you to take your chosen issue or situation through the following four-step process to develop a strategy for addressing and resolving this issue (example follows):

- After having experienced the results of using humility by way of expressing gratitude, consider how the quality of seeking humility through gratitude might play a part in your long-term strategy.
- Second, bring forward the characteristics of servant-leadership and your plan from the end of chapter 14. Apply your chosen characteristics to your issue or situation by explicitly making connections between those characteristics and the issue.
- Third, fold in the method of appreciative inquiry by identifying strengths you possess and have demonstrated in similar past situations that could contribute to help with addressing and resolving your specific issue or situation.

- Lastly, using the method of positive deviance, look toward others in similar situations or wrestling with similar issues to yours, but only look closer at those who seem to be handling that issue or situation successfully. Then, analyze their approach. What do they do differently with the same access to resources? How can you combine that with appreciative inquiry to capitalize on your strengths?

Once you have gathered this information, then weave all four elements together to define a specific and realistic strategy to develop sustainable communication with respect to the on-going issue or situation you have been addressing all along. Be sure to note how mindfulness, gratitude, the expression of appreciation, humility, and servant-leadership characteristics play a role in this strategy.

For example, since I chose the issue of social media addiction earlier as my example, I will take this issue through the process to model the way. Beginning with revisiting and examining what I wrote earlier, beginning with what I addressed for my example issue at the end of chapter 8, I recognize that, in taking accountability for my role in the creation of a social media addiction problem, I will have created an objective log of the number of times I check social media in a 48-hour period to create a better awareness of the extent of such a problem. Furthermore, folding in what I wrote for chapter 12, I recognize all the savored moments I potentially lose out on due to being absorbed by burying my face in a screen, rather than being mindful of the events around me. Taking this a step further, I begin developing a yearning to savor moments more, thereby producing a more positive form of motivation to commit toward resolving this issue. As this commitment develops, I then turn my attention to the four-step process of applying what I learned from the most recent chapters:

- Mindful awareness and reflection suggests that, with social media addiction, others around can be made to feel less important, ignored, and considerably unappreciated. By expressing my appreciation for those around me, seeking forgiveness for the harm social media addiction can cause, and vowing to work on limiting time spent on social media because of my appreciation for others, I am embodying the spirit of humility.
- The above bullet outlines an empathic and fully aware approach to addressing the problem, but I could also include listening as a means to promote healing among my relationships that had been previously damaged due to social media addiction. Persuasion would also contribute to reducing social media addiction by turning the persuasion inward on myself. Rather than simply telling myself to stop, I use the techniques of self-persuasion to commit to my new behaviors, rather than simply complying for the sake of others' wishes.
- In applying appreciative inquiry, I immediately recognize that two of my inherent and applicable strengths are as follows: 1) a concern for the health of my interpersonal relationships leading to an innate desire to seek out ways to improve them, which often results in being more mindful of how my actions affect others; and 2) my innate stubbornness and resolve, which usually cause me to follow through with something to the bitter end if I commit my all to finishing it. By combining these two qualities, I could discover the motivation necessary to challenge something like a social media addiction.
- Using the method of positive deviance, I could observe peers in similar situations and attempt to find at least a couple of them who seem to be able to balance the time they spend on social media. I could then interview and observe them to determine how they use their time differently than mine, as well as what differences such alternate uses of time produce in their lives.

By combining the above steps, I could then create a successful and committed short-term strategy that effectively addresses the issue of social media addiction immediately. This short-term self-intervention then paves the way for me to change behaviors and habits such that it sustains these changes in the long run.

Final Activity: Crafting a Sustainable Strategy

Step 1. Revisit, reflect on, and then summarize how you approached your chosen issue or situation at the conclusion of both Chapters 8 and 12:

_____
_____
_____
_____
_____
_____
_____
_____
_____
_____
_____
_____
_____

Step 2. Speculate on how humility, as generated and experienced through the expression of gratitude, applies to your chosen issue or situation:

_____
_____
_____

Step 3. Using the ten characteristics of servant-leadership, as you applied them to yourself at the end of Chapter 14, identify which characteristics might best help you to lead your way toward resolution of this issue or situation:

Step 4. Perform an appreciative inquiry on yourself by examining prior situations (ideally, situations that bear similarity to your current issue or situation) in which you experienced success, and furthermore, identify your personal strengths that led you to that success:

Step 5. Using positive deviance, find people in your life who can serve as mentors in helping you to discover freely available resources that you can apply to your chosen issue or situation, and identify that which will help you the most:

Now, as you complete this long-term plan for sustainable and lasting change for the better, assign yourself firm dates for completing the various stages. Go back through the five steps, and write those dates in the margins. Make those dates bold with a permanent marker, and even consider highlighting them. If it helps, tear out the pages and tape them somewhere you will see them each and every day as reminders. Ultimately, commit to following through with the plan, considering all the work that has gone into it by this point.

Epilogue

I want to seize this moment to convey my gratitude for each and every person who has read this book and committed the material contained within these pages to heart. In imagining the depth that you likely created and maintained as a result of working your way through this sometimes-difficult book, I am filled with a sense of gratitude. If you have maintained your gratitude journal in the margins of this book as instructed (and as I periodically nagged), you now have a list full of joy and life, and I encourage you to go back through now, to read each and every item you penned in the margins. By doing so, you may realize the sheer magnitude of what you have created here, and it is my hope that you will continue maintaining such a list. If you'll recall from an earlier discussion of statistics on those who maintain gratitude journals, your level of happiness will continue to increase all the way up to the six-month mark, leveling out at about a 10% total increase, and then it will continue to rise at a slightly slower rate, though continue to rise it shall.

One reminder I find important to bring up is that mindfulness, which has been the core of this book, is a learned skill. Much like a language or proficiency at a sport, without regular practice, you will lose what you have gained during your journey through these pages. So, continue to practice regularly. It takes little more than 15 minutes a day and a devotion to maintaining a commitment to living a mindful life to remain present in much of your daily life. I realize I am likely biased, but mindfulness changed my life by deepening my relationships, increasing self-awareness, and ultimately, providing me with a greater sense of self-control and reduced instances of mindless, automatic behavior. In the introduction to this book, I stated the following goal:

> By the end of this book, if you have done each and every activity mindfully, then you will have grown and developed tremendously as a communicator, but more than that, you will be able to see tangible, visible, even measurable results immediately.

That stated, I implore you to examine yourself to determine whether we have successfully reached that goal together. If you aren't certain, then I encourage you to talk with a loved one with whom you interact regularly, preferably over a nice meal, and ask that person if she or he has noticed any changes in you since you began working your way through this book. If you are anything like me or the thousands of students who I've taken along the same journey over the years, there will be very real, tangible differences that may not be as apparent to you since they occur slowly over time, but are readily noticeable to others.

Expert predictions with respect to the advancement of technology are that the prevalence of information sharing and distraction will only continue to intensify the Age of Distraction. Therefore, it behooves us all to seek balance in our lives and the occasional respite from the craziness of the modern technological world. It is my hope that these pages have provided inspiration for doing just that. Remember to continue employing the tools you have gleaned from this journey, for your quest to become a better communicator, friend, family member, significant other, coworker, leader, or simply a better all-around person doesn't end when you close this book for the last time. The strategy you just wrote to address and resolve your chosen issue was only practice. Keep using that template to enact further change with respect to other areas of your life.

In the end, I want to let you know that, in writing this book, I have learned as you have learned.

I often wonder which of us—reader or author, teacher or student—benefits more, but then I remember that self-improvement in the arena of interpersonal relationships is a contest in which everyone wins.

If you have reached this point in the book, I sincerely thank you, and I hope that our mutual benefit is something we experience for generations to come.

CPSIA information can be obtained
at www.ICGtesting.com
Printed in the USA
LVHW02s0557210418
574065LV00002B/3/P